OUT THERE

ALSO BY
DARRYL PINCKNEY

High Cotton

OUT THERE

MAVERICKS
OF BLACK
LITERATURE

DARRYL PINCKNEY

The Alain LeRoy Locke Lectures

BASIC
CIVITAS
BOOKS

A Member of the Perseus Books Group

Published by Basic*Civitas* Books,
A Member of the Perseus Books Group

Designed by Brent Wilcox

A cataloging-in-publication record for this book is
available from the Library of Congress.
ISBN 0-465-05760-8

First Edition

02 03 04 / 10 9 8 7 6 5 4 3 2 1

Contents

PREFACE

~

I HAD BEEN WORKING FOR SOME TIME on a collection of essays about African American literature and U.S. society in the twentieth century when I was invited to give, in the Alain LeRoy Locke series at Harvard's Du Bois Institute, the talks printed here. The stipulation was that I had to come up with something new, something I was not already at work on that would be published elsewhere. These talks became a kind of dreaming, of looking ahead to a subject I would one day like to pay more attention to: that of the presence of nonwhites in Europe.

Out There: Mavericks of Black Literature—
the title is one of convenience, because independence of vision, a willingness to live out
aesthetic choices, personal destinies, are quali-
ties of temperament we might value in any
modern writer. Ezra Pound said that most
artists fail not from lack of intelligence but
from lack of character. When we talk about
black writers, especially those from the past,
we are, as if by definition, speaking of writers
either predisposed or forced to go against the
grain. But it is useful to remember that blacks
as a people can exert just as much pressure on
the individual to conform as any other social
group, and that some of the black writers we
are now happy to claim lived and worked
among us without much honor. What I really
mean by mavericks, here, is that each of the
three works I talk about has a striking eccen-
tricity of purpose.

J. A. Rogers, born in Jamaica in 1890, published his first book in 1917 but is mostly remembered as a pioneering journalist of the 1930s and 1940s. Vincent O. Carter, a native of Missouri, is an obscure character who went to Switzerland to write in the 1950s and died there sometime in the 1980s. Caryl Phillips, born on St. Kitts in 1958 and brought up in England, is an acclaimed contemporary figure in the full flush of his writing life. They are from different times, different places, and the work of one has little in common with that of another. But in these books each describes an obsessive's solitary journey and tells a tale of alienated consciousness. Rogers's *Sex and Race* is meant to be a far-reaching history, but it has elements of travel writing; Carter's *The Bern Book* involves a tour through postwar Europe; and Phillips's *The Atlantic Sound* visits the faded ports of the Triangular Trade. They are nonfiction works that engage the experience of blacks in the United States, the place of Africa in the imagination of black people born outside Africa, as well as the history of blacks in Europe.

Rogers is from an age governed by doctrines of white racial supremacy. He argues in *Sex and Race* that Western societies are racially mongrel in their origins, that there is no such thing as a pure white race, and that his research in European sources demonstrates that before the slave trade Europeans knew this. Rogers is something of a forerunner in the field of study concerning Africa's influence in Europe, but because of his emphasis on the contribution of black people to European and American societies, rather than on the worth of Africa's civilizations, he became somewhat obsolete during the rise of black nationalism. Carter's odyssey in the days of the G.I. Bill is entirely personal. He attempts to escape the limitations of life as a black man in the United States through the dream of cultural assimilation in Europe, but, unlike Baldwin, he refuses to give up on his dream to discover a black identity. His rueful attitude toward his being black means that, most likely, a contemporary black audience would not find him sympathetic. Phillips, though hostile as an Afro-European to Europe and its history, nevertheless takes an antiromantic view of Pan-Africanism and the pieties of spiritual return to Africa. He finds his liberation from European culture in the pluralist reality of the United States rather than in pursuing a sense of belonging to Africa.

Individualistic, and not necessarily mainstream in their aims and conclusions as they confront Europe and the consequences of the African diaspora, these works reflect their periods and, in so doing, also remind us of lost episodes in the assertion of black cultural history.

The Bern Book was a gift from friends. I'd not heard of it before. Susan Sontag, Robert Boyers, and Peg Boyers found a copy of it in the Lyric Bookshop in Saratoga Springs, New York. But I can't look at some books without remembering the thrilling dust of the second-hand bookshops or the promising clutter of the small bookshops where I found them, shops like Henry's The Gryphon up on Broadway or Jill and Pat's Three Lives down in the Village. I think of these bookshops and their consolations in this time of Manhattan's great sorrow.

1

J. A. Rogers

I N *FROM SEA TO SEA AND OTHER SKETCHES,* Rudyard Kipling is taken by police on a tour of Calcutta vice. In one disreputable street he sees a European-looking woman leaning against a doorpost. The police tell him that she is the widow of a soldier and the mother of seven children. "She is a rather pretty, slightly-made Eurasian, and whatever shame she may have owned she has long since cast behind her," Kipling observes. But then a "shapeless Burmo-native trot" calls her "Mem Sahib." Kipling becomes vehement. "Her life is a matter between herself and her Maker, but in that she—the widow of a soldier of the Queen—has stooped to this common foulness in the face of the city, she has offended against the white race."

The police don't share his indignation. He is from up country and doesn't understand, but "there are any amount of that lot in the city," they tell him. "Then the secret of the insolence of Calcutta is made plain," Kipling says. "Small wonder the natives fail to respect the Sahib, seeing what they see and knowing what they know. In the good old days, the honorable directors deported him or her who misbehaved grossly, and the white man preserved his *izzat*."

However, in another sketch from the same series, Kipling is abandoned one afternoon by a trolley and is charmed to find himself in the middle of a respectable Eurasian community. Dhurrumtollah, he says, may be the Hammersmith Highway of Calcutta. It is full of "the People of India," hundreds and hundreds of them, and they are neither "Hindu nor Mussulman—Jew, Ethiop, Gueber, nor expatriated British." They are Eurasian, Eurasian families, couples, and groups out walking. Papa in a shining black hat fit for a counselor of the Queen, Mama in silk, followed by their straw-hatted, olive-cheeked brood. Young men smoke cigars and carry themselves "lordily," young women in wonderful dresses have either baskets or prayer books.

The Englishman came to India, the natives were there in the first place, but these people, Kipling says, were made in India. He says that no one has done anything for these people except talk and write about them, but then he says that they are unexploited, almost unknown material. He can think of only one novel with a Eurasienne heroine and she comes to a sad end. The one Eurasian poet he knows of, Henry Derozio, chose not to write about his people. Therefore, Eurasians needed a writer from among themselves "who shall write so that men shall be pleased to read a story of Eurasian life; then outsiders will be interested in the People of India, and will admit that the race has possibilities."

Had Kipling found so many Eurasians in London, along the Thames, instead of in a Hammersmith-like corner of Calcutta, would he have been so solicitous? The widow of a British soldier as a Eurasian prostitute is an insult to the white race. Perhaps her existence explains too clearly the origins of those Eurasians whom Kipling praised as a great discovery, the People of India. Certainly, when he regrets the aloofness of the Englishman, he is not thinking back earlier than the Sepoy Rebellion, the terrible moment when the honor of the Empire and the sanctity of white women became one. Before the Sepoy Rebellion and direct rule from London, in the days of Warren Hastings and the East India Company, Englishmen proudly displayed their Indian wives, their begums and maharajah's daughters.

From Sea to Sea and Other Sketches, published in 1900, is composed of reports that Kipling wrote on his way from his birthplace to England, by way of China and the United States, in 1888. They were for publication in his newspaper in India, the *Pioneer*. Perhaps he treats some of his reports as fiction, because the element of reportage in them is so strong. He hadn't wanted to publish *From Sea to Sea* but had little choice, as he saw it, because of the proliferation of pirate editions of his uncollected writings. He was internationally famous and vulnerable, in those wildcat days, to copyright infringement.

In "American Notes," the last section of
From Sea to Sea, Kipling is in California, a
fairy tale of deep-chested women and well-
built, elastic young men, a fairyland for the
children of what he sees as a Darwinian exer-
cise, the California Gold Rush. In San Fran-
cisco, Kipling observes that

> The Chinaman waylays his adversary,
> and methodically chops him to pieces
> with his hatchet. Then the press roars
> about the brutal ferocity of the pagan.
> The Italian reconstructs his friend with a
> long knife. The press complains of the
> waywardness of the alien. The Irishman
> and the native Californian in their hours
> of discontent use the revolver, not once,
> but six times. The press records the fact,
> and asks in the next column whether the
> world can parallel the progress of San
> Francisco. . . .

Now, let me draw breath and curse the negro waiter, and through him the negro in service generally. He has been made a citizen with a vote, consequently both political parties play with him. But that is neither here nor there. He will commit in one meal every *bêtise* that a *senllion* fresh from the plow-tail is capable of, and he will continue to repeat those faults. He is as complete a heavy-footed, uncomprehending, bungle-fisted fool as any *mem-sahib* in the East ever took into her establishment. But he is according to law a free and independent citizen—consequently above reproof or criticism. He, and he alone, in this insane city, will wait at table (the Chinaman doesn't count).

He is untrained, inept, but he will fill the place and draw the pay. Now, God and his father's fate made him intellectually inferior to the Oriental. He insists on pretending that he serves tables by accident—as a sort of amusement. He wishes you to understand this little fact. You wish to eat your meals, and if possible to have them properly served. He is a big, black, vain baby and a man rolled into one.

A colored gentleman who insisted on getting me pie when I wanted something else, demanded information about India. I gave him some facts about wages.

"Oh hell!" he said, cheerfully, "that wouldn't keep me in cigars for a month."

Then he fawned on me for a ten-cent piece. Later he took it upon himself to pity the natives of India. "Heathens," he called them–this woolly one, whose race has been the butt of every comedy on the native stage since the beginning. And I turned and saw by the head upon his shoulders that he was a Yoruba man, if there be any truth in ethnological castes. He did his thinking in English, but he was a Yoruba negro, and the race type had remained the same throughout his generations. And the room was full of other races—some that looked exactly like Gallas (but the trade was never recruited from that side of Africa), some duplicates of Cameroon heads, and some Kroomen, if ever Kroomen wore evening dress.

The American does not consider little matters of descent, though by this time he ought to know all about "damnable heredity." As a general rule he keeps himself very far from the negro, and says things about him that are not pretty. There are six million negroes, more or less, in the States, and they are increasing. The American, once having made them citizens, cannot unmake them. He says, in his newspapers, they ought to be elevated by education. He is trying this, but it is likely to be a long job, because black blood is much more adhesive than white, and throws back with annoying persistence.

When the Negro gets religion he returns directly as a hiving bee to the first instincts of his people. Just now a wave of religion is sweeping over some of the Southern States.

Up to the present two Messiahs and a Daniel have appeared, and several human sacrifices have been offered up to these incarnations. The Daniel managed to get three young men, who he insisted were Shadrach, Meshach, and Abednego, to walk into a blast furnace, guaranteeing non-combustion. They did not return. I have seen nothing of this kind, but I have attended a negro church. They pray, or are caused to pray by themselves in this country. The congregation were moved by the spirit to groans and tears, and one of them danced up the aisle to the mourners' bench. The motive may have been genuine. The movements of the shaken body were those of a Zanzibar stick dance, such as you see at Aden on the coal-boats, and even as I watched the people, the links that bound them to the white man snapped one by one, and I saw before me the *hubshi* (woolly hair) praying to a God he did not understand. Those neatly dressed folk on the benches, and the grey-headed elder by the window, were savages, neither more nor less.

What will the American do with the negro? The South will not consort with him. In some states miscegenation is a penal offence. The North is every year less and less in need of his services.

And he will not disappear. He will continue as a problem. His friends will urge that he is as good as the white man. His enemies—well, you can guess what his enemies will do from a little incident that followed on a recent appointment by the President. He made a Negro an assistant in a post office where—think of it!—he had to work at the next desk to a white girl, the daughter of a colonel, one of the first families of Georgia's modern chivalry, and all the weary, weary rest of it. The Southern chivalry howled, and hanged or burned someone in effigy. Perhaps it was the President, and perhaps it was the negro—but the principle remains the same. They said it was an insult. It is not good to be a negro in the land of the free and the home of the brave.

Our man Kipling, explainer of faraway places and distant peoples, our guide through that city of dreadful night where the white and the nonwhite are not in their ordained places.

J. A. Rogers spent some forty years digging around in the literature and the libraries of the United States and Europe for precisely this kind of dirt, evidence, testimony. His mission to inform black people of their true place in Western history turned into a bibliophile's crusade of exposure and correction and conservation. Popular black newspaper columnist, historian of Negro achievement, polemicist against white supremacy, apostle of amalgamation, sleuth in the archives of interracial sex, Rogers was self-educated and he published all his books and pamphlets himself.

Joel Augustus Rogers was born in Jamaica in 1883. He migrated to the United States in 1906, became a citizen in 1917, and that year, having had no formal education, he published *From "Superman" to Man,* a bold and unexpected discussion novel in which a Pullman porter is drawn into a debate with a white passenger on the question of the superiority of the Anglo-

Saxon and the inferiority of the Negro. The porter, Dixon, is widely traveled. He learned Spanish in Cuba and the Philippines, as an agent for a wine merchant, and his French comes from a semester and a half at Yale and from a job as valet, then secretary, to a gentleman interested in social and cultural issues. The gentleman died suddenly in Bordeaux, by which time the United States had entered the war. Dixon joined up and came home with the troops. He's seen something of the world, and knows how to serve his customers.

A Southern senator, dressed in pajamas, comes into the smoking car where Dixon is on night duty. Dixon has been reading a volume of cultural anthropology, Finot's *Race Prejudice,* which locates the beginnings of the doctrine of white racial superiority in the fractured, post-Napoleonic Germany of the nineteenth century. He tries to deflect the senator's curiosity. He's already heard the senator holding forth in the bar and in the dining car about the "niggers" and the hypocrisy of Yankees. Dixon's diplomacy frustrates the senator's condescension to a Negro who reads and who therefore must think he's as good as a white man. He challenges "George," the name by which all Pullman porters were known. He wants to know if "George" believes that a Negro can be the equal of a white man.

Since he began to study, Dixon has been amazed at the number of books in various fields in libraries, those that he could enter, that purport to prove the inferiority of blacks to whites. His answer is unsatisfactory to the senator who, because of his "color vanity," as Rogers calls it, can't believe he isn't having the last word. He insists that Dixon elaborate. Dixon is ready for him. As the Iowa prairie and then the Rockies race by, Dixon methodically bombards the senator with references to distinguished thinkers and scientists and observers who refute in their works the notion of race superiority. He has a seemingly bottomless fund of citations from other works that support the idea of the innate equality of the races. Huxley, Blumenbach, Burke.

He carries a morrocan-leather notebook and all night long he hits the senator with "Zamenhof, the inventor of Esperanto, in his paper before the Universal Races Congress, says: . . . " Or: "Count M. C. de Volney, author of *The Ruins of Empire,* says: . . . " Or: "The *Chicago Evening Post* of Oct. 11, 1916, speaking editorially of the discoveries at Nepata by Dr. Reisner of Harvard, says: . . . " Or: "Cicero, writing to his friend, Atticus, said: . . . " Or: "I have a quotation here from the *Medical Review of Reviews* for July 1916 . . ." Or: "You will find that in the 'Social Evil in Chicago,' published by the Vice Commission of Chicago, pages 97–98, 3rd edition, 1911." And: "Schopenhauer, in *The World as Will and Idea,* says: . . . "

Dixon quotes Whitman, he quotes the director of the National Museum in Rio de Janeiro; he talks about syphilis, segregation, King Mtesa of Uganda, cannibalism during the Thirty Years War, the massacre of whites at Cape François, Haiti, in 1791, and the Bible. The senator can't resist; his admiration for Dixon is set free. Their relationship becomes more personal as they look together at a newspaper story about a lynching. This senator, who had boarded the train with the conviction that the Frenchman, the Jew, the Spaniard, and the Dago were also niggers more or less, this senator who told "George" crude jokes about "the nigger" because he had the social freedom to do so, reaches his destination, Los Angeles, a converted man. He tells Dixon that he has an interest in a studio and would like to make a film from some of the history he has learned, so that more white Americans may see how narrow their views are.

Though the two characters are convincing on Rogers's terms, *From "Superman" to Man* is more essay than fiction, a strange passion play of pedantry. Rogers would revise his novel over the years, in order to cram more and more "facts" into Dixon's notebook, especially the sex research of Havelock Ellis and Iwan Bloch. In the 1920s, he toured the United States, reading from his novel, selling copies as he went. Perhaps he also offered for sale at his lectures two pamphlets: *As Nature Leads* (1919) and *The Ku Klux Spirit* (1923). He was self-made, our man Rogers, and he was vulnerable to the power of nickels and dimes.

Rogers was also an early member of the Harlem Renaissance, and he is represented in Alain Locke's *The New Negro* (1925) by "Jazz at Home," a striking essay on the lowly origins and wide appeal of jazz. But, as we learn from Arnold Rampersad's biography of Langston Hughes, Rogers did not always approve of the aim of some Harlem Renaissance writers to make the black lower classes the subject of their work. He was part of the critical attack on Hughes's poetry collection of 1926, *Fine Clothes to the Jew,* dismissing it in his column for the black newspaper *The Pittsburgh Courier* as "piffling trash" that left him "positively sick." This is odd, given the interest he would soon show in the history of prostitution.

Rogers went to Addis Ababa in 1930 to cover the coronation of Haile Selassie for the *Courier*. He reported on the Italian-Ethiopian War in 1935 and issued another pamphlet, *Real Facts about Ethiopia*. For a long time, until the Civil War dispatches of Thomas Morris Chester were published, Rogers was thought of as the first black war correspondent. He wrote for both black and white magazines in the 1920s. The *American Mercury* was of special importance to him. But his association with the black press spanned four decades. He wrote for the ordinary middle-class black, the schoolteacher, the post office worker, the Pullman porter.

As a columnist, Rogers provided a wide variety of news and information for the black community, and he was accustomed to being accepted as a trusted source in that era of Jim Crow. Rogers had, like his audience, a defiant interest in the subversive ironies of blacks in world history, ancient and modern. However, the books Rogers wrote after *From "Superman" to Man* seldom figure anywhere these days. That is partly because they are what used to be called Negro history. They are illustrated books for a general audience, and as such they have long since been superseded.

His titles are unmistakably those of an autodidact, and they are also for a popular audience: *World's Greatest Men of African Descent* (1931); *100 Amazing Facts About the Negro* (1934); *World's Great Men of Color, 3000 B.C. to*

1946 A.D., published in two volumes in 1946 and 1947, then reprinted in 1972 with an introduction by John Henrik Clarke; *Nature Knows No Color Line* (1952), described as an exposition of Negro ancestry in the white race; *Africa's Gift to America* (1959), in which he talks about black American heroes such as the cowboy, Deadwood Dick; and *Five Negro Presidents* (1965), as in, Did you know that Warren G. Harding was a Negro, or at least he would have been legally defined as such in the state of Louisiana? These books can be seen as preparatory to or offshoots from his most ambitious project, *Sex and Race,* a three-volume survey of the history of race mixing that Rogers began to publish himself just as the United States entered World War II.

Sex and Race, a survey of retribution, a study in trying to beat the white man at his own ideological game, was Rogers's life work. Dixon's cherished sources in *From "Superman" to Man* are recycled in *Sex and Race*. The project was obviously on Rogers's mind for a long time. In "Jazz at Home," he has visited the racially mixed cabarets of Montmartre and seen the interracial student couples of Montparnasse. He was, at this time, already engaged in his reading about Negroids and Negritos as the first people, about Western Europe as a terminal region of prehistoric migration, about the Mediterranean basin as the home of Aurignacian man before he either disappeared or was absorbed by others in the Ice Age.

His reading about race mixing among the ancients and his compiling of sources having to do with the suppressed histories of black people in Europe introduced him to the higher tittle-tattle of court memoirs as cultural history, as in, Louis XIV's lonely queen had a child by her Negro dwarf. The dwarf disappeared, and the mulatto daughter was spirited away to a nunnery for the rest of her life. Rogers returned to Europe in 1927 for three more years of trawling in the libraries and museums of England, France, Germany, Italy, and Spain. In the mid-1930s, he was back for a few more years of scouting and scouring. In the late 1950s, he, over seventy years of age, was still at it, interviewing black and white American troops in Europe.

All that time, he was working up the German historians on ancient Egypt, on who was on the throne when the Great Pyramid was built in the Fourth Dynasty, on the art of the Fourth and Fifth dynasties, on the invasions of Esar-Haddon of Assyria and Alexander the Great. He sought to learn about the *Rig-Veda*, Dravidians, and the racial origins of the caste system in India. He was not forgetting to check out books on aborigines. Then he wanted to consider what the books of the Tcheu-Li had to say about a diminutive people with black and oily skin in southern China in 122 B.C., not to mention an article from the *Bulletin* of the Catholic University of Peking for 1930, "The Importation of Negro Slaves to China under the T'ang Dynasty, 618–907 A.D.," by Chang Hsing-lang. He treated every book as a door, and maybe at times it was hard for him to hold at bay that Lewis Carroll feeling.

It has to be said that much of *Sex and Race* is a mess, but as a compendium of quotation and anecdote it is a mess without precedent in black literature. Rogers's argument in *Sex and Race* doesn't advance so much as it accrues through more than a thousand closely printed pages and hundreds of illustrations. Rogers has footnotes galore, often as mere emblems of scholarship, and a no-frills, not-much-help index running to some twenty-seven pages. His earlier books are much more composed, and perhaps there was no way Rogers could sustain anything like a style over the long stretch that is *Sex and*

Race. It is impossible in a short summary to give a sense of its detail and density, its frantic touching of all the bases.

The rise of fascism turned his early purpose of moral restitution for black people through recognition of their true history into the monstrously all-debts-settling one of seeking to establish, to bring to light, to make people realize, and even to prove, that the earth is populated for the most part by mixed-race peoples, that race mixing has been human practice since prehistoric times, that race mixing is the reality of history.

That the three volumes of *Sex and Race* are a scrapbook, a quilt, a patchwork of reference and quotation, is perhaps fitting, because, as Rogers contends in his introduction to Volume I, *The Old World: Negro-Caucasian Mixing in All Ages and All Lands,* published in 1940, race theory in the Western world is made up of scraps, much like Frankenstein's monster.

The scraps used in the construction of race theory were taken from the Bible, from Lincoln, from slave dealers, ignorant divines, prejudiced travelers, bad historians, mixed-up ethnologists, and twisted craniometrists. Rogers invites those who think him a lunatic to reconsider the books on race that had been accepted as science. The remembered and the forgotten—Gobineau, Thomas Dixon, Madison Grant, Lothrop Stoddard, Houston S. Chamberlain, Hans Guenther, R. W. Shufeldt, Henri Champly, and the subscribers of the *Victoria Society Journal*—they were the witches around the cauldron making the hell-broth boil. "Finally the monster stirred to life," Rogers says. "His name: Adolf Hitler."

World War II was a race war, in Rogers's view. People don't go to war over religion anymore, he says too confidently. "Hitler's Aryan has announced that he is 'the master race, destined to rule the world.' He is looking down on the Anglo-Saxon much as how the latter looks down on the Negro. In a word, he is calling the Anglo-Saxon 'nigger.' . . . German propagandists are declaring that white Americans, after cohabiting with Negroes for centuries, are a Negroid people, and are bringing their Negro strain into the British Isles." In September 1939, Lord Haw Haw was broadcasting the allegation that Churchill's father had Negro blood. It was an act in a propaganda war, Rogers concedes, but for him it's always worth investigating these accusations. After all, cousins of King George VI, the Mountbatten marquises of Milford Haven, have Negro ancestry through their descent from Pushkin's daughter. He never said his black pride couldn't be snobbery.

Racism, Rogers maintains, is a function of trade and colonial expansion, and was therefore recent as a doctrine in European history, and not representative of what Europeans had always thought of black people in their history. People are not like the branches of a tree, going out from the trunk and never mingling again. Europe is only fifteen miles from Africa, whereas the New World is three thousand miles from it. If blacks could go far, then they could travel near as well. Rogers quotes Thomas Huxley, H. G. Wells, liberal contemporary and eighteenth-century German anthropologists to the effect that Europeans could not possibly be considered representatives of a pure race. The good guys also include Albert Payson Terhune, Franz Boas, Ruther Benedict, Melville Herskovits, Jean Finot, Arnold Toynbee. And Schopenhauer, the hero of *From "Superman" to Man,* believed that whites were dark people who'd lost their color somehow.

Rogers begins with Europe, because his primary target is the Anglo-Saxon in the United States. Perhaps that is why he seems to enjoy rubbing in the point that Jim Crow and the Nuremberg Laws sprang from the same impulses. Though he refers to Du Bois's histories and sociology, Rogers uses the work of white writers and historians, because he didn't want his findings to be discounted as the projections of wounded black pride. Rogers goes continent by continent, country by country, to discover that no land, apart from Japan, was able to resist the allure of Negroid or Negro soldiery.

It is difficult for the nonspecialist to judge Rogers's anthropology, because it is so much of its period, Europe in the 1920s, though in an appendix he brings us up to Leakey. But, then, so too would a classicist today be more skeptical than a lay person of how Rogers reads mythology. Zeus is an Ethiop in one source. Aeschylus says of the union of Zeus and Io, "And thou shall bring forth black Epaphus." This was myth's way, Rogers tells us, of saying that they were of mixed race. Greek mythology, Judaism, Christianity, Islam—Tacitus thought the Jews originated in Ethiopia and Rogers is off. He turns over the Bible, to exonerate Cain, Abel, and the land of Nod. The Koran gives him the tradition that the first disciples of Muhammad were Negro and he's off again.

We get names in Volume I, a daunting plenitude of names. He reaches far back, to Homer, who speaks of the woolly hair and sable skin of one Eurybiates. He dashes forward to say that recent excavations on Crete prove that the origins of Greek civilization were Egyptian. (By the way, the Phoenicians were Negroid, too.) Herodotus, who called the people of Mesopotamia and India Ethiopians, said that black doves flew across the water and founded the oracles at Dodona and Delphos.

We get Hippocrates, Theodectes, Aristotle, Heliodorus, and the poet Asclepiades (270

B.C.), who sings of his black love, "Coals are black; but when they are alight, they glow like rose-cups." Ovid makes it clear that Sappho was not considered white by the ancients. "If I am not fair, Andromeda, the daughter of Cepheus, was swarthy though the complexion of her country was pleasing to Perseus. White pigeons, too, are often mated with spotted ones and the black turtle-dove is often beloved by a bird that is green," she says to Phaon in Ridley's translation of Epistle XV of the *Heroides* of Ovid. Rogers doesn't leave out Pope's translation: "Brown as I am an Ethiopian dame."

Rogers also wants us to know that Hannibal's army was thirteen years in the Italian peninsula. Rome defeated Hannibal with the help of a Numidian king, Massinissa. Plutarch mentions Alexander's black general, Clitus Niger. Then there are Suetonius, Terence, Lucian, Martial, Juvenal, St. Jerome, and Shakespeare's *Titus Adronicus,* in which the Goth queen is said to be in love with Aaron, the Negro. He doesn't bother to be chronological. It's as though he'd glued down the index cards marked Ancient World in the order that they tumbled from his satchel. His point is that the ancients in Europe knew about blacks and that they also knew of whites and blacks doing what people do, mixing and matching. But the hard part, the area of learning where the intrusions of the untutored are most resented, is over.

Rogers is less intimidated when talking about North Africa in the Middle Ages. The historical references on this subject were gratifyingly obscure in the days before people became interested again in the influence of Averroist thought on Dante. And so a book from 1863, *History of the Intellectual Development of Europe,* by John William Draper, describes the superiority of Moorish over Nordic culture in the eleventh century. Arabian literature reveals prejudice against pure blacks, but there was the great black epic poet, Antar. In North Africa, the Berbers claim descent from the Mazoi, the Negro soldiery of the Egyptian army. Moorish invaders, who brought slaves to Spain, were themselves colored and intermarried with Spaniards, who then carried this Negroid strain as far as the Netherlands.

Rogers storms through Europe, looting and pillaging, piling up his treasured jewels of information. Portugal was the first example of a "Negrito republic in Europe." Sicily is "profoundly Africanized." Napoleon's army had small, black Portuguese soldiers who were called "the fleas." Rogers cared mightily about disseminating the news that the tar brush had touched Beethoven's family. "Man kann in Beethoven s Physiognomie leicht negerähnliche Zuge finden," he quotes from Frederick Hertz's *Rasse und Kultur* (1925), one of sixteen sources he offers on the matter. His other sources, nineteenth-century biographies and memoirs of those who knew Beethoven, admit that he was swarthy, dark, reddish, brown, crinkly haired. But is this proof that Beethoven's father's family went back to a black soldier in the Lowlands? If not, then perhaps guilt by association will do. George Bridgetower, Beethoven's accompanist, was a mulatto.

The experience of reading *Sex and Race* is one of embrace and recoil as Rogers indiscriminately loads us down with the provable and the forever dodgy, the serious and the frivolous. Sometimes his footnotes, not always adequate or acceptable, tell when he was at work on a given aspect of his subject, in the way that an itemized credit card bill is a diary, a record of movement. The references go in clusters: in the 1920s, he was reading about Syria, Palestine, Arabia, and Persia;

in the 1930s, he was reading the memoirs of English travelers in Africa. Sometimes, he clearly couldn't go back to a particular library or text to check his facts again. And sometimes *Sex and Race* reads as though it had threatened to consume him, because the first-person voice breaks through in the book at times of what could be called narrative stress. "I have met in my time almost every race under the sun, and I have still found 'race' as elusive as electricity or the ether, have still to understand what the racialists are talking about. The most striking thing to me is the similarity of the psychology of the so-called races. The three principal things I notice that will move all peoples from the most benighted to the most cultured are in order named: money, a smile, and flattery. Humanity, instead of being different, is rather too monotonously alike when you get acquainted with its different 'races'."

Volume II, published in 1942, is *The New World: A History of White, Negro, and Indian Miscegenation in the Two Americas*. It involves some repetition. Once again, Europeans set sail with their biblical understandings, such as that man originated in the tropics, Rogers explains. From this realization came a profound philosophical change in the West: Instead of having fallen, man has been rising since olden times. The white clergy taught that the pre-Adamites had to be Negro, people who had no part in God's creation. How else could Cain's wife come from the land of Nod? To whites, the unknown beasts of Revelation also had to be Negroes. And of course there was Ham. The West Indians, Rogers interjects, told the missionaries and slave traders that they got the story about Ham wrong. All men were black, but when Cain killed Abel God shouted and in fright Cain turned white.

Rogers then turns to the blacks who sailed with the Spanish explorers, the slaves taken to South America, and sex and procreation among blacks, Indians, and whites in those sixteenth- and seventeenth-century days of few European women on that continent. There is a long discussion of Brazil, the most mixed country in the world, with its history of anyone who had the money or influence buying papers declaring them "white," after which Rogers travels through the race-mixing history of each South American country, from the arrival of the Europeans to the dictators of his own time, offering brief biographies of Negro heroes and villains. He then moves to the West Indies and Latin America. In his native Jamaica, the white settlers represented "the dregs" of three European kingdoms; adultery was everywhere, the clergy was immoral, and the class of unhappy mulatto heiresses included Robert Browning's grandmother,

Margaret Tittle. The Browning Society Papers of 1890, according to Rogers, tell the story of Browning's father being ejected by the beadle of the church on his mother's sugar plantation, because he was sitting with the white folk.

However, two-thirds of the volume about the New World is devoted to the United States. "God made the white man and God made the black man, but the devil made the mulatto," the colonial saying went. Rogers is convincing on white indentured servants and whites in slavery and their relation to blacks, and on the first attempt to found a doctrine of race based on physical appearance coming with the introduction of slavery into Virginia. He then goes through several states, using diaries, letters, memoirs, unleashing a hail of tidbits. For instance, Jefferson Davis's mistress was his niece, his brother's mulatto daughter. He goes from their then to his now. George Schuyler, that other obsessive, collected much of the material Rogers uses on intermixing in the South. Pity the poor prodigy, Philippa Schuyler, brought up in her own Jack 'n Jill version of the Skinner Box, because of the genetic vanity of her interracial parents.

Rogers is sometimes too trusting, or willful, and takes the attitude, when it comes to stories of a notable person having black blood, that there would be no smoke if there hadn't been a fire. It does not always suit his purposes to admit that a politician's enemies weren't above spreading rumors about his Negro ancestry, although he has a very good time defending the university official who lost his job after he wrote about Warren Harding's Negro cousins in Ohio. Editions of the unfortunate academic's work were rounded up, brought to Washington, and burned, Rogers asserts. In spite of its flaws, Volume II has much more authority than the preceding volume, because of the abundance of convincing documentation available to Rogers.

In Volume III, *Why White and Black Mix in Spite of Opposition,* published in 1944, Rogers writes in separate chapters about the attitude of scientists, politicians, and the clergy toward mixed marriages. In chapters such as "Is Vehement Rejection of the Negro Man by the White Woman Sincere?" "Which is More Beautiful, White or Black Skin?" and "Color Attraction and Homosexuality," he sounds almost gleeful. He presents supposedly objective information about which race, white or black, was or is more sexually "competent," in both ancient and modern times. Guess. Taking off from his beloved Schopenhauer's *Metaphysics of Love and the Sexes,* he even presents his own explanation of the "psychologic and cosmic forces" behind the urge to breed interracially, and finds that Jefferson predicted the inevitability of the United States' becoming a mixed-race nation. In Volume III, with its case histories, Rogers's transformation from historian to a sort of Reichian visionary of the interracial orgasm is complete.

The force of purpose, the grand design, is evident; so too are the compromises his limited resources imposed on him, and the presence of the undermining element of wish fulfillment as scholarship. The eye can't be trusted, Rogers warns us in Volume I, but then he sometimes appeals to the reader to trust his or her eye or, better, the experience of J. A. Rogers, when it comes to the business of deciding who is a Negro or is of Negro ancestry. "I met in Harlem a Negro woman of unmixed ancestry, who resembled strongly Amenophis II, the great Egyptian conqueror." The climate of his times helps to explain. In his day, Egyptologists and ethnologists didn't agree on what was a Negro. Some ethnologists classed Ethiopians as white. Right-wing ethnologists never find evidence of Negroes in the oldest graves in Egypt, 5000–3600 B.C., because the type of ape-like Negro they're looking for only exists in their imaginations, Rogers complains. But Rogers files another complaint at the beginning of Volume III, and in so doing makes an admission that he doesn't seem to realize is damaging to his project.

"Certain orthodox scholars, white and colored, have not liked the history as given in the two preceding volumes of *Sex and Race,*" he says. He corrects the false reports. He never said that Julius Caesar, Handel, or Einstein, for instance, were of Negro ancestry. He accepts that in some instances he has been wrong, but doesn't specify which. Instead, he reminds his critics that he has had to work alone for years, with no staff, no philanthropic or academic affiliation. He feels that he has been ridiculed by established scholars, because they believe that if they do not know his sources, then such sources could not possibly exist or have value. He asks how any one person could know everything about the eight million printed items in the National Library of France.

He turns on Gunnar Myrdal, who produced *An American Dilemma* in 1943, aided by seventy-five experts, at a cost of $209,000, and paid for by the Carnegie Corporation:

On page 1393 of this book (1st ed.) I am listed as an example of those who write "pseudo history, fantastically glorifying the achievements of Negroes." On what grounds was this judgment arrived at? On anything I had written? No, I was judged on a non-existent book—a book that no mortal could ever have seen. Here are the facts: In 1927, I finished a manuscript entitled, "This Mongrel World, a Study of Negro-Caucasian Mixing in All Ages and All Countries." At about that time I was asked to fill out a blank for

"Who's Who in Colored America," and in-
tending to publish the manuscript soon I
listed it as being published. However, cir-
cumstances prevented my doing so.

Rogers explains that he used this work as
an early draft for *Sex and Race,* then threw the
manuscript away. He continues:

> Nevertheless, this non-existent manuscript
> is listed as a published book in Myrdal's bib-
> liography. What had happened? In reading
> through my biographical sketch in "Who's
> Who in Colored America," Myrdal, or
> some of his assistants, saw the title and on
> that alone condemned me. Not a word was
> said of any of my published books. They
> probably didn't take the trouble to look into
> any of them.

Perhaps Rogers thought of *Who's Who in
Colored America* as a place to advertise. After

all, his books have advertisements in the back and sometimes order forms.

This Mongrel World is still listed in the bibliography of the 1997 Transaction Press edition of *An American Dilemma,* but the only reference to Rogers in the index calls him simply a "Negro" historian. It seems a small thing, but it doesn't help his credibility for him to be self-righteous about having caught people out because of a book title he ought to have been truthful about. However, he quickly regains ground: people should ask themselves why they are so immediately resistant to his subject. Could it be that the propaganda about the Negro having no history until slavery has been too well internalized? Information is revenge only when it doesn't make one lose one's balance.

Rogers's countryman, Claude McKay, thought him a little mad. What McKay called the Negro elite hadn't liked *Fine Clothes to the Jew* and it didn't like McKay's novel, *Home to Harlem* (1928), any better. Rogers declared it obscene in much the same language Du Bois used for *Nigger Heaven*. In his autobiography, *A Long Way from Home* (1937), McKay is snide, though he doesn't give Rogers's name. McKay's agent gave a champagne party in Paris in 1928, when anybody who was somebody was over from Harlem.

> Thus I won over most of the Negro intelligentsia in Paris, excepting the leading journalist and traveller who remained intransigent. Besides Negro news, the journalist specialized in digging up obscure and Amazing Facts for the edification of the colored people. In these "Facts" Beethoven is proved to be a Negro because he was dark and gloomy; also the Jewish people are proved to have been originally a Negro people!

The journalist was writing and working his way through Paris. Nancy Cunard's *Negro Anthology* describes him as a guide and quotes him as saying he had observed, in the flesh market of Paris, that white southerners preferred colored trade, while Negro leaders preferred white trade. Returning to New York, he gave lectures "for men only" on the peepholes in the walls of Paris.

Maybe Rogers gave different lectures, depending on his audience: one for the Negro librarians, another for members of the Boulee. The reference to Nancy Cunard's *Negro* is appropriate. Not only are Cunard and Henry Crowder much talked about in *Sex and Race,* Rogers's work itself is reminiscent of *Negro* in its ambition to be comprehensive, to answer all the questions. Legal segregation in the United States was, among other things, a pantomime about hypocrisy, and perhaps the tabloid audacity in *Sex and Race* reflects his sense of his audience's exasperation with what whites didn't know about themselves, about whites and blacks and sex.

In *Black Odyssey: The Story of the Negro in America,* published in 1948, Roi Ottley describes the restricted opportunities for black writers provided by the Negro press, and cites Rogers as "perhaps the only writer who made both a living and reputation almost solely among Negroes. . . . His books, *Sex and Race,* and *The World's Greatest Men and Women of African Descent,* have had extraordinary appeal to Negroes." Sutton E. Griggs, the self-published writer at the turn of the century who tried to combat race ideologies in his novels, couldn't survive on the little his black audiences offered him. Rogers kept on.

However, when Rogers died in 1966, the traditional Negro press seemed increasingly like something from the second-hand life of segregation. In that era of repudiation of things Negro, such as hair-straightening advertisements, the long-standing features, topics, and voices of the Negro press were sometimes dismissed as part of the status quo, of what had been wrong. Few had sympathy for someone who had been a young man back when amalgamation was a topic of strenuous debate. It wasn't color snobbery or high yellow panic. To point to the reality of amalgamation was to argue that segregation, that the legislation and judicial opinions that were putting Jim Crow into place, would accomplish little in the end. In persecuting us, you are persecuting yourselves. But even before the publication of *From "Superman" to Man,* the most influential black intellectuals had come to the conclusion that in order for the Negro race to advance it must not be "absorbed."

Moreover, by the 1960s the angle of approach in cultural history shifted, at least on the

black side of town, so to speak. We don't need
to claim Beethoven. We have our music and it
has an African history. The discussion wasn't
with Rogers's sources anymore. When Stokely
Carmichael proclaimed Black Power to the
Mississippi night, Rogers looked obsolete, this
old man obsessed with what the round heads
and long heads, the silky haired and the frizzly
haired, had been doing together since they
emerged from the fog of history.

Between 1916 and 1954, William Leo
Hansberry lectured at Howard University
on "The Cultures and Civilizations of Negro
Peoples in Africa." A recently published volume of his notes, *Africa and Africans as Seen
by Classical Writers,* edited by Joseph E. Har-
ris, overlaps with Rogers. Hansberry makes
no mention of his popularizing contemporary, and Rogers doesn't seem to have been
aware of Hansberry. Martin Bernal mentions
neither. In writing about Rogers in 1972,

John Henrik Clarke called attention to those books in that first wave of Black Studies that validated some of Rogers's claims: *Blacks in Antiquity* by Frank Snowden or *The African Genius* by Basil Davidson. And Rogers is cited in Ishmael Reed's celebrated novel of Neo-Hoodooism, *Mumbo Jumbo* (1972). More recently, in her excellent study, *White Women, Black Men: Illicit Sex in the Nineteenth-Century South,* Martha Hodes follows trails once taken by Rogers, trails to sources once considered suspect, too subjective, for real historiography.

What a project for an enterprising, well-funded student: to track down Rogers's examples and footnotes. What images were removed from churches and museums in Italy following the declaration of the purification laws of 1938? Are all the images of the Black Madonna in Eastern Europe the result of centuries of smoke? Which Medici palace has in

its collection that Bronzino portrait of Allesan-
dro de Medici, son of Pope Clement VII and a
Negro servant? Rogers claims that a painting
by someone called Verlat, *Christ and Barrabas,*
is in Antwerp and that it depicts the blackest,
most Negroid Christ he'd ever seen. Benizet
and the monumental volumes of *The Image of
the Black in Western Art* do not give his name.

Back in the nineteenth century, black
American travelers in Egypt didn't doubt that
they were gazing upon the relics of a once-
great colored civilization and some black
evangelists, such as Jarena Lee, held that Jesus
was colored. Disapproved of, underground,
alternative, vernacular learning—this itself
has a long history. Cleopatra and the tawny
question, the darkening of the Ptolemies
question, the glamour in the attraction of
these questions just won't go away. Africa is
everywhere, both the nightmare and the
dream proclaim.

Notes

1. After this talk, Richard Newman of Harvard University shared with me the information about Rogers contained in a very informative article, "The Bran of History: An Historiographic Account of the Work of J. A. Rogers" by Valerie Sandoval, in *The Schomburg Center for Research in Black Culture Journal* (vol. 4, no. 4, Spring 1978).

2. Karen C. Dalton of the Image of the Black in Western Art Project at Harvard University has pointed out to me that some of these lines of inquiry have indeed been followed up. Dalton mentioned Mario Valdes, who is at present engaged in research much like Rogers's: "Alessandro de' Medici's Patronage of Portraiture" by Frank Martin, a master's thesis submitted to the Art History Department of Hunter College in 1990; and her own "Art for the Sake of Dynasty: The Black Emperor in the Drake Jewel and Elizabethan Imperial Imagery," in *Early Modern Visual Culture: Representation, Race, and Empire in Renaissance England,* edited by Peter Erikson and Clark Hulse (Philadelphia: University of Pennsylvania Press, 2000).

2

Vincent O. Carter

AN UNPUBLISHED MANUSCRIPT IS
like a message in a bottle, floating,
floating, waiting to be found. A forgotten
book is much the same, lost in the strong cur-
rent. Vincent O. Carter is the author of
both—the unpublished and the long out of
print. Some thirty years ago, in 1970, the John
Day Company of New York published *The
Bern Book: A Record of A Voyage of the Mind* by

Vincent O. Carter, a strange, disquieting, sometimes gorgeous account of what it was like for him to be the only black man living in Bern, Switzerland, between the years 1953 and 1957. Why Bern? Carter claims the Bernese themselves want to know and this work is his attempt to answer them.

In his introduction, Herbert R. Lottman, an editor who knew the author of *The Bern Book*, tells us that Vincent O. Carter was born in Kansas City, Missouri, in 1924, and that Carter had told him his childhood was the happiest and most beautiful part of his life. His family was poor. Carter worked in a defense plant before serving in the army. While waiting to be demobilized, he spent a year at Oriel College, Oxford, but couldn't pass the exams, and so went back to Kansas City to work as a third cook on the Union Pacific Railroad. Two years later he entered Lincoln University in Pennsylvania. After graduation, he had a job at an auto plant in Detroit and did graduate work at Wayne State University. Soon after that he went abroad, and ended up in Bern, the capital of Switzerland, a city of civil servants, "a parlor of convenience for the nations of the world," as Carter describes it.

Lottman says that he's read two of Carter's unpublished—and perhaps unpublishable—novels. The first, The Long Green Way, he characterizes as a literary experiment, as if Joyce had rewritten *Buddenbrooks*. We think: Oh dear. The second, The Primary Colors, about Carter's childhood in Kansas City, won Ellen Wright's enthusiasm, but eleven U.S. publishers rejected it between 1963 and 1968. Carter had worked on this second novel for ten years. It was 275,000 words long in its first draft. Before he read Carter's novels, Lottman says he thought of fiction by blacks as another form of journalism. But Carter "didn't seem to protest enough. He had dedicated his life to art, to the exclusion of social comment. And a black writer who, even when he uses his own life as a theme, does not stay within the accepted bounds of 'Negro fiction' is a difficult person to place." We think: The picture is coming into accusatory focus.

Evidently, Carter wrote *The Bern Book* before or around the same time as his unwanted fictions, because Lottman speculates that publishers perhaps don't know what to do with Carter's "miscellany turned art," implying that the manuscript was making the slow rounds. But at least one publisher knew what to do with it. The book exists, in libraries or second-hand bookshops. Lottman warns us that, as with Carter's fiction, a degree of difficulty is involved in *The Bern Book*, beginning with how to take the way it "straddles accepted literary genres." It is *The Anatomy of Melancholy* for this century, he says; it is digressive, like Laurence Sterne; it is quixotic. It is neither travel writing nor autobiography. It is Swiftian. Lottman finishes by saying that Carter was still in Bern, subsisting on odd jobs. Word was that he had stopped writing altogether.[1]

Carter says in his own two-page, deliberately obscure and cloaking introduction that his "Reisebuch" records his change in attitude,

the transition from that state of mind in which I considered myself innately different from other people (by which I meant "white" people) to one in which that difference disappeared only to embarrassingly reappear in the form of a new and more subtle illusion, that of myself as a distinct entity as differentiated from all other entities; and more, the further transition to that state of mind in which my newly discovered distinctness (which I doted upon) proved to be the greatest illusion of all, and I was finally revealed to myself to be (but only in rare visionary moments) merely a state of mind, a mere thought of myself; which condition I shared with all others in the universe!

This realization, I say, was inspired by my travels. The scene of my partial metamorphosis (which is still going on) in the city of Bern—the object upon which I focused my attention, giving and taking from it those fragmentary impressions which cast some light upon my own identity.

Maybe Carter's publisher had suggested that some kind of preface would help to convince a postassassination audience of the relevance of this Eisenhower-era work. Maybe our coming to this book is like calling on someone who is thrown that his invitation was taken seriously. There is much apologizing and disclaiming and stashing of socks behind bookshelves as the guests are ushered in.

Seventy-five short, shortish, and long chapters make up the 297 pages of *The Bern Book*, chapters given titles such as "The Foundation-Shattering Question," "Personal Problems Involved in Answering the Question," "Why I Did Not Go to Paris," "Why I Left Amsterdam," "Why I Was Depressed and Sunk in Misery," "A Portrait of Irony as a Part-Time Job," and "A Little Sham History of Switzerland, Which Is Very Much to the Point, and Which the Incredulous or the Pedantic May Verify by Reading a Formal History of Switzerland, Which I Have Certainly Never Done, and Will Probably Never Do." This narrator, Carter, is indeed descended in part from the squiggly line in *Tristam Shandy*.

Carter tells us that his destination is selfhood. He is unwilling to work, though not to work is a violation of one of the Ten Commandments of Switzerland. But he is afraid for his writing and for himself if he worked. His heart is filled with the religion of high art. He must give all his time and concentration to becoming a writer and no writer, he says, can work from a fragmented self. Carter is prepared to suffer in the pursuit of his dream, like the great men of literature in their garrets, but he does not want to be thought conventionally bohemian, not even when he's had too much to drink and is singing on the streets.

Then, too, the jobs he could get, he says, would put him on display. He is already tormented that people stare or point at him in the street. Drivers almost have accidents when they spot him. He complains that in his neighborhood his every move is known. He's so visible, so different. Perhaps for Carter, remembering the factories back in the United States, a menial job would not suit his new dignity and status, voluntary outsider, expatriate writer, ambassador from that other world. He seeks to reinvent himself by shedding that generalized identity imposed on him by the fact of his having been born black in the United States in favor of an individual identity granted by geography and, more importantly, by his efforts as a writer.

The Bern Book, which at times reads like fiction, but mostly like the diary of an isolated soul, also keeps score of the stories sent back by American magazines, of the rejection slips mounting in a drawer in the room he can't pay for. Now and then Carter reflects balefully on life back in the United States, on the history of blacks in the United States, but only because this unwanted subject has followed him like the ghost in the service of Dido. But *The Bern Book* isn't a work of memory. It is a work about ambivalence, escape, evasion, and the expatriate's creed of noble procrastination, noble withdrawal. Carter is that familiar, defensive figure in the café, the man who refuses to be practical, the artist with impossibly high standards, the stranger who is difficult to help, the black man who attacks the white friends who have just fed him or from whom he has just borrowed money.

His bouts of self-deprecation, of feeling ridiculous and guilty, are touching, but they are compensations for a refusal to be candid without the protective coating of facetiousness. The very gratuitousness of the project, of being, as Carter occasionally reminds us, "a hypersensitive nigger" and yet sending himself out into the Swiss streets for experiments in "lacerating subjective sociology," points to everything he can't bring himself to say. Late in the work, Carter mentions that blacks, African and American, have come through town, but they haven't stayed. He is dripping with contempt for the fuss Bern makes when Haile Selassie arrives on a state visit. Otherwise, he is the only one, and that is an effortless, if headachy, stardom. The Bernese are too polite to ask why he who is so passionate about jazz and books doesn't head for a metropolis, London or Paris, where there are loads of artists, blacks, and other black American expatriates. Obviously, he wants to have that exclusive position, and believes that he can clear his head while occupying it.

In the first chapter, "Since I Have Lived in the City of Bern," he is with new Swiss acquaintances one evening at a table in a Mövenpick, a chain of German-style cafés, fielding what are, to him, intrusive questions of why he, of all people, came to Bern, of all places. He has been in Bern some three-and-a-half years, but there is always someone new to ask the question. New whites, a new audience. He is trying not to resent his new acquaintances, so he claims, and embarks instead on eloquent, ironic complaint about how the Swiss only get to what they want to know in roundabout ways. "He has never or seldom met a real black man before. He has, however, heard much and wondered much. He knows or has heard one or three Negro spirituals and he is an ardent jazz fan." No, Carter replies coldly, he's not a musician; no, he's not a student.

The accidental information that Carter has an appointment the next day at two in the afternoon, when most of Bern is at work, leads to the admission that he is a writer. But this disclosure causes a retraction, a pattern often repeated in *The Bern Book*, a tendency that goes with the advance and retreat of the narrative itself. Carter makes his interlocutors, as he calls them, guess what he writes, what kind of stories, then where they can read his stories, which are sort of about love. Alas, Carter hasn't much to show for his three-and-a-half years in Bern other than to indicate the pitch of his ambition. He imagines that they are "struggling with Goethe and Rilke and Gotthelf and Harriet Beecher Stowe and me." As one of the Swiss inches toward

"the hated question"—"Why did you come to
Bern?"—Carter reflects:

> It all depends on who is asking it, the tone of
> voice in which it is asked and the aura of
> what light is gleaming in his eyes. It depends
> upon whether or not there is a smile upon
> my inquisitor's face, and what kind of smile.
> It depends upon my peculiar feeling of secu-
> rity or insecurity, which is very much influ-
> enced by the weather and by my metabolic
> rate on that particular day. And finally, it de-
> pends upon whether or not I will have to
> spend my last centime for the wine.

Carter settles into a circuitous explanation
of how he ended up in Bern, an explanation
with plenty of interruptions for metaphysics
of a kind and for much forehead wiping, as
the waiter in the Mövenpick eyes how little
they are drinking at his table, how much

room they're taking up as the dinner hour nears. Carter is telling us a story about the stories he has told others. Great swathes of formal prose are in quotation marks to remind us that this is a repeated conversation. It takes a while to decide when Carter is being satirical in a deadly vein, because he doesn't ever seem accustomed to the idea of us, the readers, in spite of the asides, the authorial appeals.

Are you Protestant? Catholic? Jewish? Atheist? Are you rich or poor? Could you be by any chance the son or daughter of divorced parents? Did your mother conceive you one moonlight night behind sweet-smelling lilac bushes in the park, as a result of which conception your father forgot to marry her?—are you a bastard? Are you thought to be a little stupid? And as a result are you a little maladjusted? Are you too tall?—too fat? Did your mother and father drop you on some sadistic stranger's door-step at three a.m.? If you are a war refugee trying to become established in a foreign country, if you suffer behind the iron curtain or in front of the lace one, if you have flapping ears or buck teeth, if you're a blue-eyed boy in a brown-eyed family, I am speaking to you. Are you working as a dishwasher when you should be living the life of a millionaire? Are you the son of a minister? The insignificant son or daughter or brother or wife or husband of a great member of your family? Perhaps you are intelligent but merely lack sensibility? Or are perhaps too sensible? Are you English now that the value of the pound has diminished and the sun is beginning to set upon the British Empire? Do you have Communist worries? If you have any of these petty little problems you will be able to understand, or rather feel, what I shall say about the effects of the word "nigger" upon my consciousness. I cannot speak for the other fourteen million Negroes in the United States.

His satirical moments, though powerful, are few.

He'd had beautiful experiences as a soldier in France. "Lada da da da" was back in 1943. Ten years later, he'd saved enough money to return, with the intention of getting a crummy room in the Quartier Latin. "What succulent agony hadn't Balzac, Hugo, de Maupassant suffered in the Faubourg St. Germain!" He imagined an old bed, a table with a candle, a fireplace gone to pot. He dreamed of eating cheese, drinking red wine, smoking hashish, and immortalizing his decadent mistress in his stories. "I shall suffer. . . I consoled myself, squeezing my fat little imitation leather wallet of traveler's checks in twenties and fifties."

However, upon arrival he discovered that instead of being the great liberator of ten years earlier, he was just another tourist with luggage to inspect. He had trouble finding a hotel, because he was taken for a North African. When he did find a crummy room with a naked yellow ceiling bulb, he was told that he had to apply an evening in advance to bathe and that he would have to pay extra for it. On top of that, he could hear the couple above him in bed. He saw "American go home" scrawled on walls. He endured it for a month, until one evening he was in a bistro, complaining about having been overcharged for his Pernod. A Frenchman in uniform followed him out, agreeing that Carter had paid too much. The French were thieves and cutthroats, Carter told him. The Frenchman protested as he introduced himself, a wounded soldier recently returned from the Tunisian campaign who was waiting for his wife, a medical student. The wife, when she arrived, looked half-starved, but had, Carter notes, "large clear courageous eyes." Though he had just eaten, he accepted the soldier's invitation to have supper with them in their home.

Where they lived reminded him of the slums he was born into. Rats and roaches were in garbage pails, the smell of urine and decayed food was on the stairs. In the room of the soldier and his wife were a little green bird in a wooden cage and the wife's brother, a poet with the same clear, courageous eyes. The three slept in the one bed. On a wooden box was a gas burner and on the blue flame a tin can of dirty gray soup. Carter's host made him take the one chair in the room. There were only two plates and two spoons and one cup. The poet brother, obviously hungry, waited until the couple and their guest had eaten. To hide his feelings, Carter talked too loudly and smiled too much. But he failed to hide from the serene, knowing eyes of the wife his embarrassment "due to the glaring irony of my obviously prosperous condition as compared to theirs." The three thousand dollars in traveler's checks in his pocket were a dreadful weight as he sipped the dirty soup and occupied the only chair. Shortly afterward, he fled Paris.

A similar scene occurred in Amsterdam. He found a room with a Dutch writer and his wife, a ballet dancer. In the darkness, through the curtain, he could hear them making love with abandon. One day, when he lamented to a beautiful young lady the plight of the Negro wandering through the world like a child without his mother, she remarked, "They made soap of my parents." "'The Germans.' She said the word quietly, as though she had said, 'The Potatoes.'" "I had seen the smile, which now skirted the periphery of the faces in this room, upon the faces of Negroes when speaking of incidents which occurred during the race riots in Chicago and Detroit, or when they spoke of lynchings in the south or police brutality in the north."

The crisis for Carter in Amsterdam came when out walking with a Dutch graphologist who shared his reverence for Spinoza. The graphologist pointed to a house and said: "My family was taken there. They were all killed."

At the sound of his voice I stopped suddenly and tried to shake off the oppressive feeling that came over me. . . . How could he tell it, ten years later, I wondered. Why to me! Why tell that horrible mess to me! His voice droned in my ear, rehearsing the details until I felt like spitting in his face. . . . As we walked, I thought: "He confesses to everyone because he didn't declare his identity and die with the members of his family. . . . He associates me with himself because I am a black man. . . ." I experienced a sensation of pity mixed with nausea at the thought of him; not because of what he suffered but because I perceived that he derived some perverse pleasure from telling the intimate details of the death of his family, from the pain which he inflicted on himself and others.

Carter fled Amsterdam, thinking of Descartes. The invisible fires of Nazism, Judaism, Catholicism, and Puritanism were kindling at his feet. "I felt anxious about my condition in the world. Danger was everywhere."

In Munich, he found the address of a former classmate who was there to study medicine; because the American schools were so crowded, there was scarcely room for "legitimate citizens," much less Jews, Chinese, Japanese, Indians, and Negroes. But Carter's friend had left Munich abruptly. His room was still littered with the broken glass of a brawl he'd had with a Jewish American student. Minorities, Carter observes, under pressure from the majority group, sometimes fight out of self-hatred, fear, or the violent passion of an inexpressible love. Carter's friend, he learned, had fallen apart "like a wet pretzel." Professors and students were uncooperative, studying in a foreign language was difficult, and few white women would have anything to do with black men, though Carter knew American Negro soldiers during the war and in the peacetime army who married German women and either took them to America—"heroic," he exclaims—or never went back themselves.

In a large beer hall, a beer stadium, he corrects, a woman who looked as though she'd been painted by Frans Hals put her hand between his thighs. He nearly vomited. But his free-floating anxiety lessened as the train pulled out of the station. An old thrill stirred within him, that of being on the move, headed for some new place. "When I was a child it was always tomorrow which held the promise of whatever that something was which I always wanted but could not have today. . . . Perhaps that is why romantic and mysterious things have always played such an important part in my life. . . . What will I find in Bern?"

But in Mövenpick, the waiter's face wears an angry scowl and Carter tells his companions that he must go. "Friends—a Mr. and Mrs. C . . . have invited me for fondue. Mrs. C hates it when anyone is late for one of her fondues, for which she has acquired quite a reputation, because if it is not eaten immediately after it reaches its point of perfection, it spoils, the cheese clots into globules of chewing gum. And! Since I have no money with which to eat elsewhere, gentlemen, I hope you will excuse me in favor of another time." This invitation for fondue out in the suburb of Wabern, fondue he must walk fifty minutes for or take the tram to when he has the money, will turn out to be something of a leitmotif.

He begins the first of many wistful strolls. After a while, when he's completely broke, walking will be one of the few things he can do to amuse himself. "Oh how I miss my own rosy window in the evening! How I miss my pork chops, fried apples and brown gravy. . . . I shall always be in some strange city, looking through the windows of other people's houses, eating at other people's tables." Moreover, he is dissatisfied with his answers to his interlocutor in Mövenpick. "I had merely said to that young man what I said to those young men who were like *this* instead of like *that*, one of *these* instead of one of *those* types. I was grateful. . . . not to have been confronted with one of *those* types, because they are bastards."

To explain what one of those types is like, Carter summons the image of a clever young man who reads American newspapers, speaks foreign languages with a good Swiss accent, the sort who wants people to know that he's interesting. He has met everyone, and is curious about the exotic specimen. Consequently, he is overly familiar, "Hi, Wince," or "Hellow, Winsen!" One of *those* types says to Carter, "What! You still 'here' in Bern? I don't see how you can stand it."

I looked up at this gentleman with a murderous expression in my eyes. I looked up at this gentleman with a murderous expression in my eyes because on this particular day there was a melancholy humor in the air. I had just received a rejection slip from a magazine whose reader had assured me that: "The rejection of your story does not necessarily reflect upon its merit, but merely means that it was not suitable to the needs of our magazine." I was spending my last sixty centimes for a beer with which to wash down that last little nuance. On top of that summer was fading. I had felt it just that day, between half past three and four thirty while standing on the little boardwalk overlooking the dam where the river diverts into a channel behind the Schild clothing factory and opposite the Schwellenmatteli sauna and tearoom. Down there I had wished that I were younger and that there had been more sun this summer. I had regretted the changes which red leaves, then no leaves, cold wind and snow would bring into my life. What is to become of me? I had asked myself, looking down into the frothy volumes of ice-cold blue-green water: Do I have what it takes to be a writer? . . . Do I have what it takes to jump? The water looks appealing. If only it weren't so cold! . . .

"Why don't you come home?" my mother had just written: Your cousin has a wife, a nice job and a nice little house and a doghouse and a dog. He earns eight thousand a year now. You could easily do as well with all your education and travelling experience, etc. . . ."

Let's complicate it:

My last story wasn't very satisfactory. I had to rewrite it. But I hadn't written in a long time—about a month, perhaps two — time goes by so fast! Perhaps it was even longer than that since I had written. I had read a lot of good books and even the fact that their authors were dead afforded me no special satisfaction. Twenty times that day some contentious person, some noisy sadist, had asked me with an eerie smile, "How's the writing coming?" And I had replied:

"Oh, it's coming . . ." wondering when? How? Feeling useless and ridiculous because of the clean white block of paper in my briefcase.

"Sold anything?" my well-wisher asked before I could say I had someplace to go.

On this particular day while my man, one of *those*, was wondering how I could stand it in Bern, I owed three months' rent and four coffees at the Rendez-vous tea-room. I had borrowed all that I dared from everyone I knew to borrow from. My friends sped by when they met me in the street. I was a little hungry. I had friends who would feed me but I could not go to them that night because I planned to go to them the following night. The pile of un-published manuscripts at home gave me no satisfaction, nor did I enjoy reveling in the misery of Edgar Allen Poe and Mozart, a favorite pastime which I usually reserved for the gloomiest days. That day, as sum-mer slipped into autumn, I thought of home, of my mother and father, of my youth and of my plans and ambitions. I thought of the love of a woman and of the domestic life. I had regrets. Doubts overwhelmed me. As I sipped my beer in the Bali I grasped at the last philosophical straw in the hope that it would prevent me from drowning.

Then he attacked me:

"Hi, Wince!" or "Hel-low, Wincen!" he cried above the wrangle of the piano and the glare of the gaudy lights and the nervous laughter of the decoleteed barmaid, extending a sticky hand. "What's new! I'm surprised to see you!" Had he not seen me when he spoke to me as he was leaving the Sultan tearoom not less than twenty minutes ago? "What! You still here in Bern? I don't see how you can stand it!"

I looked up at this gentleman with a murderous expression in my eyes. I took the measure of his weak chin. . . .

On such days, there is no limit to Carter's sensitivity. It is the proper artistic posture, but his stomach churns when he hears the word "Neger," because of its similarity to the word "nigger."

So conditioned were my ears to that sound that the nuance from "nig . . ." to "Neg . . ." was reduced to negligibility. For "nigger" had become for me a word which was more than a word. It was an animate being which I had invested with a royal if demonic distinction. It was a sort of Satan of words, with its own retinue of Satanically noble words, such as: "black," "kinky," . . . "flat nose," "thick," "lips," "thickliptips," "red," "bright," "light," "white," "dark," "darky," "blue," "blues," "sing," "happy," "dance," "child-like," and countless others, so many that I could fill volumes with examples of their spellbinding powers. I could give accounts of marvellous feats which they are able to perform, such as leaping into the foreground of my visual field from the anonymity of the printed page of a newspaper and bewitching me out of my self control."

Much of his time in Bern is spent in looking for an affordable place as a lodger. The Bernese have heard various things about the Negro, the black, the African, including a story bashfully told him by a proper young girl of how white women who go to bed with black men risk becoming locked in a fatal embrace. They are liable to become martyrs to the orgasm. He does not contradict her. In time he learns how not to intimidate nervous landladies. Of course things never work out. He will not conform to the house schedule; they are unreasonable.

Eventually, he finds a room in the home of an elderly couple in a beautiful district, the Kirchenfeld, and his period of greatest hope begins. He takes his meals with them. They are sincere, open. The wife becomes his confidante, and though he says they can't find a common language, they do talk somehow, according to him, about everything, from the stupidity of McCarthyism to the inevitability of his loneliness. He is desperate for a Guinivere. A pretty girl unfailingly passes into view when he is on the verge of an epiphany, as if to say, Is not a pretty girl an epiphany? The landlady listens to his disappointments over love affairs and over affairs that never got going because he doesn't want to date a girl who won't let him pick her up at her home, or introduce him to her family, or meet him in public, in broad daylight. Meanwhile, the traveler's checks run out. Poverty forces him to move, but a new room in a new neighborhood is an unknown world for Carter to describe and thus to lose himself in.

Another spasm of hope comes to him when he sells to Radio Bern a feature on his impressions of the city. The staff treats him as a colleague after a while. But the flowers of hope fade. His relationship with Radio Bern turns awkward. They don't want too many features on Negroes and when they do, they want spirituals, and not too much jazz. The "innocent conservatism that always stereotypes the Negro" upsets him. He argues with them about the superiority of disciplined expressions of Negro music over the undisciplined and untrained. He prefers Marion Anderson to Mahlia Jackson. Anderson's voice represents "the acme of what Negro expression can reach." His trump card is that he is more of an authority on this question than they. He is the first Negro his Swiss friends at Radio Bern have met, so he is astounded that they assume they know so much about what they call "the deepest sentiments of the Negro," "the primitive simplicity and rhythmic intensity of Africa."

However, his argument about the difference between fine or pure art and folk art, the difference between the primeval outburst of songs by Negro laborers in the Alabama fields and the finished expression of lieder is as much a received, inherited idea as the stereotype he opposes, even though, to make sure that his position isn't racially exposed, he contends that Louis Armstrong at his best is qualitatively the equal of any classical master; that Ellington may be compared to Stravinsky; and that Lionel Hampton has moments of "terrible tension" that recall the effects of Beethoven. "How does one classify the virtuosity of Art Tatum?" At least he goes on to poke fun at his "pedantic, argument-crushing discourse on art."

"You are ashamed of this music because you are ashamed of your own people. You are ashamed of being a Negro," one of his Radio Bern colleagues remarks. His heart pounds. "How unreasonable you are . . . because I refuse to accept what seems to me to be a noisy insincere rendition of the Negro spiritual. . . . Perhaps I am ashamed of the Negro people . . . of being a Negro. Heaven knows he has caused me enough trouble. He's so black and controversial." He offers a discourse on the origins of the spiritual and the work song, which means bringing in Spinoza and Shakespeare. But he loses, he says, his clarity. He can't write about a subject he's too close to. Maybe what bothers him about the spirituals is that they were written when the Negro was a slave, he says, almost with a sigh. Throughout *The Bern Book* Carter redeems his pompous tone by admitting to what does not flatter him. As soon as he utters something incredibly high-minded and arch, his rhetoric is stalked and silenced by the low thought, the honest thought.

He is up against his pride, his inhibitions. With much mock heroism, he finds the courage and humility to give English lessons. He also takes small parts in plays when a

Negro is required—either Balthazar at Christmas or, in a Max Frisch play, a Negro oyster vendor who gets killed in the first act. A story in a Swiss women's magazine, a few programs for Radio Bern—such things give him some validation as an artist. More often he is addressed as Herr Carter, which makes the sound of Der Neger less odious to him. Friends tell him that his difficulties in Bern aren't because of racial prejudice, but just because he isn't Bernese. He realizes that he has overcome his distaste for being stared at. The supposedly unwanted stardom of being the only black in town has been made bearable by a dash of success. When he pauses to let a couple pass through a door before him, he thinks of the good impression he's making. He can be respectful, because he has won for himself a measure of respect "over here."

The children of his new neighborhood stop playing monster with him and take him for granted. It has taken him a long time to get accustomed to how they do things "over here" as opposed to how people do things "over there." But acceptance brings disenchantment, because he is still subject to the vicissitudes of the expatriate's improvised, precarious, lonely existence. To merge with a crowd is a consolation. "No city silence is ever so still as that of the city of Bern at twelve o'clock and one o'clock and two o'clock, on a Monday, Tuesday or Wednesday night, or any night during the Christmas week when all the families huddle in rose-tinted rooms behind heavily curtained windows. . . . I have walked under the low arches of the old town and heard the water purling between the intermittent sounds of my footfalls! How lonely the electric lights seemed with no company save the blind stones!"

He communes with Bern during long, private hours of concentrated observation.

I had seen the city at four a.m. and at six a.m. I had heard the first streetcar rumble down the street and beheld with wonder from the center of the Bahnhofplatz the last magical moment when all the streetcars stood in the station filled with the home-bound who had been to the movies or to the tearooms or dancing or to choir rehearsal, strolling or working late, huddled in a tight little group under the strain of a pleasant fatigue when the moon shone and a warm breeze wafted them on: waiting—having boarded now the streetcars, paid and pocketed their transfers—for the signal, a short blast of a whistle. It blew! As the bell in the tower of the Evangelical church rang, all the cars moved silently in the eleven directions from the heart of the city, while the buses coughed and whined through the shifting crowd of pedestrians which dispersed like sparks of fire before the wind.

When he's not under the covers in a new cold attic room, or sparring with the people who have just given him a free meal, he is in the cafés. His favorite is the Rendez-vous. It is his clearinghouse of ideas, the social space where he is most like everyone else. Even so, he follows the comings and goings at the Rendez-vous with a bitter, yearning intensity. He becomes so involved in imagining the pasts and various fates of the waitresses, in analyzing the geisha-like relationship of the Swiss waitress to the Swiss businessman, in pondering the neglect of the businessmen's wives, that his Benjamin-like physiognomy of the coffeehouse opens out into a full-blown critique of Swiss society. Swiss women, in the 1950s, did not have the vote. "Switzerland is a man's world."

Timid, bourgeois, security-obsessed, insurance-wrapped, bank-ridden Bern, Switzerland. He blames Switzerland for not nurturing its creative artists, saying that Klee had to go elsewhere to make his name, evidently not considering that the art market was in New York, Paris. He devotes pages to the expectations of the average Bernese, the prospects of the young men, why the young men sometimes don't marry the young women they meet in the coffeehouse, what kind of girls they do marry once they are promoted; he speculates as to why there are so many homosexuals in Bern; he scrutinizes the lives of pensioners, widows.

When he first arrived in Bern, the city was celebrating the six hundredth anniversary of its independence, the day when the canton joined the Swiss confederation. The costumes, the prancing steeds, and heraldic banners dazzled him. The festivities transported him back to the books of his childhood. He'd come, asking the city for sanctuary. Then, when he was broke, he became the "migrant mendicant," asking the city to take care of him. Because they possess the world, he says, he'd always expected more of rich people, meaning white people.

After nearly four years, his blackness has worn off as a novelty and he himself can become indignant at the new buildings and other changes in the city. He can go on about the Föhn, the depression-causing air pressure of the region. Bern belongs to him at last. He is territorial, having demystified the city, cut it down to size, turned the scrutiny away from his worry of what they think of him to his insistence that Bern hear what he thinks of its virtues and shortcomings. "Am I not the only black man in this place?" The result is the same as in the United States, he says. "I am isolated from the people." He means that he is still cut off from the kind of people he wants to know—white people. We cannot know for certain if when back in his hometown he considered himself among but not of black people. He is also telling us that the passage of

time has robbed him of his theme, his innocent stardom—that head-turning blackness.
They were his whites. He'd trained them.

As for the selfhood that was the object of his
quest, his finding it depended on a break with
things "over there." In Kansas City, he didn't
choose the life he led. He was "a dwarf among
apparently normal-sized people. Accordingly,
I had dwarf-sized loyalties, aggressions and
fears—both real and imaginary." In the ancient Swiss city, his stature has increased, he
says. He's still a dwarf, but one in three-
leagued boots. He can move about freely, exposed. And yet some mysterious convention
dictates that he must mind when he's noticed.
He's willing to put himself through a great
deal to move to what is in effect an idealized
white neighborhood. The new life in the literary Promised Land: smelling and tasting
essences, he calls it; being overwhelmed by a
respect for the unknown; finding the narrow

streets interesting, seeing faces from Old Master paintings in the faces of passersby. This is the flanêur's creed, this is the romance of Europe in the era of the G.I. Bill Negro.

He has come to take the cure. A whole continent of white people with other problems. "I had to leave the nigger in the woodpile to take care of himself." In one scene, Carter describes a second visit to Paris during which he gambols through the rusty grass of the Bois de Boulogne. Forget me, forget me. On second thought, forget me not. And what better place in which to purge himself, to empty himself and start over, than in neutral Switzerland, haven of refugees? English was not yet universal in Carter's Europe, that postwar place of scarcity, cold water, and strong cigarettes, an occupied place very interested in the evidence that the world's most powerful democracy didn't practice what it preached. Carter's concluding attempts to have an insight about

"Nothing at All" and "All Is Nonsense" are political only in the sense that he is talking, in the absurdist style of the period, about the cold war and the atomic bomb. This was also Stalin's Europe.

In one of his hopeful moods, Carter buys ribbons for his typewriter and paper clips. He has with him works by Dante, Goethe, Gide, Eliot, Donne, Nietzsche, Flaubert, Plato, Montaigne, Kant, Hegel, Faulkner, and English-German, English-French, and English-Italian dictionaries, the syllabus of the believer.

> The mountains glowed with an intense amber coloring, which was washed in whiteness, against an equally intense vermillion sky; but only for an instant, because it deepened after that, the amber softened into degrees of red and then pink and blue, as musky hoar-mists rose from the floor of the valley until the mountains appeared as

a vast jagged range of blue ice stained with
frost; the blueness deepening all the while
into tones which obscured the entire view
by slow certain degrees, leaving—but only
for a few indeterminate minutes—a violent
egg-yellow border rimming the horizon.

But we don't think of Rilke, we think of
those whose existence he gives no clue of knowing anything about. Their absence is one way of
identifying Carter as a black writer, given his
talent for perverse and sad ironies. Who had not
heard of *Native Son*? When did Baldwin's fame
cross the Alps? It's hard to believe that Carter's
informed and curious Swiss friends, especially
one of *those* types, wouldn't have asked his opin-
ion of the African American writers they'd
heard of in 1955, in 1957. Head under the
Kirchenfeldbrücke, not competing; head in the
clouds, not competing, especially not with—
what's his name again? What was it Baldwin

said about not spoiling another black man's hustle in a room of white people?

"I was simply a living wonder," Baldwin says in "Stranger in the Village." For him, as for Carter, the Swiss children who shouted "Neger" had no idea what echoes that sound raised in him. Their astonishment was poison to him, because he was among people whose culture controlled him, created him. No matter how friendly they were, he was a latecomer to the culture they effortlessly inherited. Then his essay glides away from the "paranoiac malevolence" he detected in the glance of some villagers toward the race problem in America, the fact that there is nowhere in America where he, a black man, could be a stranger to a white man. Baldwin's phrases ring like the moral of *The Bern Book*: "People are trapped in history and history is trapped in them." "The slave in exile remains yet enslaved to his past." "The rage of the disesteemed."

Carter grasps, as Baldwin does, the connection said to exist back then between European culture and the prestige of the Anglo-Saxon in the United States. But because this is the culture he wants to belong to, Carter finds the continuity, then discounts it, preferring to declare himself an illusion, like the landscape, an echo perhaps of *Invisible Man*. But he's not speaking for us on his bizarre frequency, and maybe not to us either. And he's not Jean Toomer out to transcend the notion of race, though Carter is from that time when one of those types maybe thought it a compliment to say something like he didn't think of Carter as a black, he thought of him as a person. Carter himself has already suggested that his being black was a sort of blemish or deformity in his own not entirely amused eyes. He who is embarrassed will one day be an embarrassment.

In 1953, Wright, Ellison, Baldwin, and Carter were writing in the same Europe. Ellison went home to mine the richness of the culture in his backyard; Wright, the existentialist, was said to have lost it by the time he died in Paris, as if every book by a great writer had to be good. William Gardner Smith married a Frenchwoman, held a French job, wrote his novels about the United States as well as Europe, and died "over here." Chester Himes got mad and maybe as a tormentor of susceptible white women he got even. Baldwin got sad and ascended into our hearts from France. Because of our interest in their fiction, we are interested in their biographies, in their diaries and letters. But in the case of Vincent O. Carter, we are presented with his diarist's impressions and self-examinations with no knowledge of what his fiction is like.

There is one scene in *The Bern Book* in which Carter relates an incident from his childhood. It shows very clearly that he could capture the look of the back stoops and the speech of where he came from. A syndrome of his times: I won't go home until I can justify my having been away. The claim of *The Bern Book* on our attention now is not Carter's reputation—he was reviewed and then filed away—and not necessarily the whimsical self-protection that *The Bern Book* contains. It's not the voyage to Laputa with the flying island attached, or even those moments where he seems to have been touched by a lonely voice from Gogol. Carter's record of a voyage of the mind is also a record of trying, trying again, and failing. We can reject him, but we must accept his failure, because failure is also part of the history of the black American expatriate writer in Europe.

Meanwhile, Carter is dependent on his hosts while criticizing them for their complacency, a not altogether grown-up position from which to hold forth. I pledge allegiance to Peter Pan. . . His childhood, he is supposed to have said, was the happiest time of his life. On those Missouri back stoops he was not yet out in the Jim Crow world. Carter, orphan of the storm; Switzerland, in loco parentis. Early on, Carter receives a letter from his mother. He cries like a baby in the middle of the Bahnhofplatz as he reads her unfinished thoughts, her loving words that only mothers use. "We're sorry but we—your father and I—just can't afford to send you any more money. We're deep in debt for what we've sent you already. You know we would if we could." She finishes, "After all, you're a man. You're thirty years old already and we're forty-six." He wasn't so spoiled that he did not know that his individuality, his emotionally luxurious flight, had been paid for by those who'd probably never heard the phrase, children of the diaspora.

Notes

1. As it turns out, Henry Louis Gates, Jr., while a graduate student at Cambridge University, journeyed with his wife to Switzerland in 1975 to interview Carter for an article he was doing for *Time* magazine on black expatriates. The interview was not included in the published article, but remains among Professor Gates's papers. It is his understanding that Carter, a physical fitness enthusiast, died in the early 1980s.

3

Caryl Phillips

HOW ANNOYED EDITH SITWELL MUST have been that night in Student House in Bloomsbury in 1932. There she was with her bald face like a Plantagenet tomb—a famous description—ready to blow up the skirts of her admiring London audience with her rude remarks about writers as famous as, if not more famous than, she. D. H. Lawrence was of the Jaeger School of Poetry, she said. Jaeger was a kind of woollen underwear. She did not think much of Lawrence's work; his novels were overrated. She said she knew of an American writer of thirty-one or thirty-two who was far finer. "I told her at once that it was William Faulkner and she rather blinked a bit."

Then the controversial Miss Sitwell wanted to repeat Lytton Strachey's put-down of a young, pushy composer who reminded him at a party that they'd met two years earlier. Strachey said over his beard that two years was a nice long interval. No, Miss Sitwell certainly wasn't going to tell her audience the unfortunate young man's name. Coy, grand Edith, sharing her insider's morsels. However. "As soon as the meeting was over I went to her and told her that I hoped I wasn't intruding, but I would be glad to know if her young composer was not Constant Lambert. You never saw a woman look so surprised. She had to admit that it was and wanted to know how in the name of Heaven I knew that."

The good lady soon found that her surprise
annotator had strong opinions of his own. He
wondered if "a genuine poet today" could
write "great poetry in the old traditional form,
the sonnet form for instance." Sitwell didn't
think there'd been a good sonnet since Keats
and Wordsworth. "Myself: 'What about Eliza-
beth Barrett Browning's *Sonnets from the Portuguese,* particularly the one beginning, "If thou
woulds't love me,"' . . . Miss S: (Shaking her
head) . . . I do not believe a woman is strong
enough physically to weight the syllables as a
man can in order to strengthen the lines'." For
her, technique was a matter of physique. Of
course she had to meet this stranger properly.
Himself was introduced and the two wound up
the evening in agreement about the weakness of
modern art. No matter how pleasing Stravinsky's music, he couldn't move one's feelings like
Bach, Mozart, Haydn, Beethoven. Those two
kidders, Edith Sitwell and C. L. R. James.

Clearly, C. L. R. James was writing this report for his audience back home in Trinidad.
Such stimulating evenings define the atmos-
phere of the student and young writers' quar-
ter where, he says, he has been living for ten
weeks. He doesn't mind saying that until he
found that lecture series in which Sitwell appeared, he'd been suffering mounting nervous strain in Bloomsbury. But once in Student House, confidently trading views with
Sitwell and Walter de la Mare, James, thirty
years old, no longer a student, was in his element. He was released. This was what the
scholarships and the years of study had been
for; this was what the rehearsals with Trini-
dadian intellectuals and British expatriate
artists in Port of Prince had been for—to arrive in London, the metropolis, the capital of
the Empire, and to find himself at home in
the literary culture. He didn't mind indicat-
ing that there had been some days of struggle,

because, in the end, he was proud to report and could assume that those interested back in Trinidad would be proud to hear that he had not let down the side.

C. L. R. James's "Bloomsbury: An Encounter with Edith Sitwell" appears in the anthology *Extravagant Strangers: A Literature of Belonging,* published in 1997 and edited by Caryl Phillips, novelist, dramatist, screenwriter, and impatient, gloomy traveler. The anthology, Phillips notes in what is for him a characteristically bad-tempered preface, grew from his dislike of an observation made by a professor in Singapore about the wave of "outsiders" whose writing had recently reinvigorated the canon in Britain. To Phillips's way of thinking, "outsiders" had been reinvigorating the English canon for two hundred years.

What is striking about Phillips's choices for his anthology is that he locates, in a manner that seems very natural for him, Rushdie and

Thackeray in the same tradition, that of the keen observer of England from the colonies—"And what should they know of England who only England know?" To present English literature as an expression of a historically diverse culture, a mongrelized culture, is a decision, a challenge, but also simply a recognition of a long-accomplished fact. However, Thackeray succeeded in becoming known as an English writer, but did Rushdie? Did he even want to?

Caryl Phillips was born on St. Kitts in 1958 and when he was four months old his parents migrated to Britain, ending up in the north of England, in the football-crazed city of Leeds, which still has one of the largest concentrations of Jewish people in the United Kingdom. Not all immigrants from Russia in the nineteenth century took ship from Liverpool for New York. Some found their way to Leeds, to work in its textile industries. After one hundred years, Leeds has almost forgotten that they came from elsewhere. Or maybe another mass emigration has distracted Leeds from them. The trouble radar moved on, on to the ship *Windrush,* which in 1948 brought Jamaicans to England in their hundreds. Phillips is a son of the Windrush generation, the term given the postwar immigration of loyal subjects from the English-speaking Caribbean who came to the mother country to make up the labor shortage. However, because he was only twelve weeks old when his parents left St. Kitts, Phillips has no memories, no experience, of that other place and the trauma of separation, if every going had been traumatic, can only be something he has been told or imagines. It is not what he remembers.

This adds some poignancy to the background of his first novel, *The Final Passage,* published in 1986, in which a nineteen-year-old woman embarks with her husband and infant son on that life-changing voyage to England. Her new beginning is portrayed as the last in a series of her chances to make life come out right. In Phillips's second novel, *A State of Independence,* the fled heart, the native son brought up elsewhere, returns and must struggle to claim his place. "Ambition going to teach you that you going has to flee from beauty, . . . Panama? Costa Rica? Brazil? America? England? Canada, maybe? West Indian man always have to leave his islands for there don't be nothing here for him, but when you leave, boy, don't be like we. Bring back a piece of the place with you. A big piece. I sick of hearing old men talking about 'When I was in such and such a place,' and 'when I was here and there and every damn place,' and they still don't has nothing. Ambition going to teach you that you going has to flee from beauty and when you gone to wherever, remember me, boy. Remember me." Phillips's underlying subject is the psychology of the migration, the founding, historical event for most Caribbean Britons, the new tribe that had been created by it. Or is it the founding event after all?

Before *Windrush* and increased immigration from the Caribbean, there was that other defining episode, the long drip of human tears, the slave trade, slaves in Britain, slavery in the West Indies. The brutality of the sugar plantation is the stuff of Phillips's novel *Cambridge;* the slave trade in eighteenth-century Africa sets the terms for the quest for identity in modern times in his novel *Crossing the River* and in the novels *Higher Ground* and *The Nature of Blood,* the horrors of being declared an unwanted stranger, a tribal threat, link the experiences of blacks and Jews, holocaust upon holocaust. These are the subjects of an interrogator of history, which, for a black writer of Phillips's generation in Britain, is not the same thing as saying that they are reflections of his formal education, apart from the Shoah and World War II. Phillips tells us that when he was growing up in Britain, his middle-class white schools offered nothing except for Shakespeare in the way of a literature in which a black youth could find nonwhites. Perhaps this is why Phillips returns so often to the figure of Othello in his work. Othello, the man for whom things go wrong precisely at the moment of his acceptance into the new society. Othello, the outsider who must be on his guard always and everywhere. Phillips is drawn to Othello's paranoia and also to his combative vanity.

In the introduction to his first work of nonfiction, *The European Tribe,* published in 1987, Phillips recalls that the discovery that a black person could sustain a career as a writer came to him on a trip to the United States in the mid–1970s. At Queens College, Oxford, where

Phillips was reading English literature, a doctor advised him, a student suffering from nervous exhaustion, to take time off. Before he hit the Little Italy, the Spanish Harlem, and the Harlem of New York, an African American friend at Oxford had told him that North America had been settled by Europe's castoffs and criminals. By the time Phillips reached California, he had been subjected to so many petty and racial insults he was nearly convinced that the moral character of whites in the United States had changed little since colonial times.

In a bookstore in a college town near Los Angeles, he came across an intriguing title, *Invisible Man*. He had an intuitive understanding of the title from his own life, but it was *Native Son* that altered forever the direction of that life. "If I had to point to any one moment that seemed crucial in my desire to be a writer, it was then, as the Pacific surf began to wash up around the deck chair. The emotional anguish of the hero, Bigger Thomas, the uncompromising prosodic muscle of Wright, his deeply felt sense of social indignation, provided not so much a model as a possibility of how I might be able to express the conundrum of my own existence. Even before I had opened Ralph Ellison's *Invisible Man,* I had decided that I wanted to try to become a writer."

Back in the Oxford lecture hall, Phillips found his appetite for theories about Shakespeare's problem plays and Milton's late poetry considerably diminished. He saw two clear paths. He could, as Derek Walcott puts it in *Midsummer,* be inducted "into white fellowships." He could pursue an academic career which, so he thought at the time, would take him even further from the majority of black people or he could take the path of no security whatsoever. Harold Cruse's *The Crisis of the*

Negro Intellectual, with its controversies about West Indians, Jews, and the Party, helped him to make up his mind. "I spent my last few weeks at Oxford resenting that it had taken America to make me conscious of my desire to write. This alone seemed to condemn the European Academy which had raised and educated me, and I found myself tediously attempting to question everything I had ever been taught." To orient himself to Britain seemed futile, which suggests that tutorials in John Webster or Jonson's *The Masque of Blackness* were no longer enough. His relation to the culture around him in those early days of British entry into the Common Market he came to view as a European question.

"Before I explored Europe there was one other journey I felt compelled to make: the journey back to the Caribbean of my birth. The discoveries that I made there were both deep and profound, but I still felt like a transplanted

tree that had failed to take root in foreign soil."
His Caribbean journey only intensified his desire to know Europe and Europeans, he says.
And so, in 1984, Phillips started out in fly-rid-
den, impoverished Casablanca. He crossed over
to nutty, jingoistic Gibraltar, went into a Spain
still recovering from Franco, and then into a
France that watched Le Pen, in spite of the official, patriotic belief that Martinique was a department of the nation.

This was the Europe of a football hooligan-
ism closely connected to neo-Nazism, a Europe of all the neon being on one side of the
Iron Curtain and gag-inducing petrol and tobacco fumes on the other. Italy before the
black-market business of Somalians selling
their work papers to West Africans; Germany
and its then disfranchised, excluded Turks;
liberal Holland and its bowed Malays. But
Scandinavia? Phillips was harassed by the authorities at Oslo's airport the week Desmond

Tutu was to accept the Nobel Prize. Damaged Poland, wheezing Russia with its tolerated and soon-to-be-abandoned children of Third World allies—history, Phillips concludes, is the prison from which Europeans often speak. "It is a false history, an unquestioning and totally selfish one, in which whites civilize and discover and the height of sophistication is to sit in a castle with a robe of velvet and a crown dispensing order and justice. When Bokassa aped it, Europe mocked simply because she could not stand to look at herself. Such history involves superiority and inferiority, so that when the Japanese, who used to be inferior, began to find a voice technologically and economically, the Arabs oil, and the Jews a country, it left Europe with only the blacks and themselves to despise." Britain had the largest colonial labor pool to draw from and was ahead of other European countries in the enactment of immigration laws.

When Phillips published *The European Tribe,* Britain did not have a single black member of Parliament. He grew up hearing and not responding to jokes in Leeds about Pakis singing "We Shall Overcome." It was the Britain of Enoch Powell. Yet it was also the time of Bob Marley and the Wailers and Linton Kwesi Johnson. Phillips describes his efforts to get in touch with that black Britain in the 1970s, how he left the "Nigger go home" scrawled next to his name on the notice board at his college, left the handful of blacks he could find university-wide, a Nigerian mathematics student here, a Rhodes scholar there, and took the train to London, where he would go from pub to pub in Brixton, trying to learn, to pick up something. Sometimes on these vague, sad trips to black London he would miss the last train back to Oxford and spend the night in a lounge at Heathrow. But he was always on time for his 9:30 A.M. class in lyric poetry.

From C. L. R. James to Austin Clarke, we can read about the education of "little black Britons." In *The Enigma of Arrival,* V. S. Naipaul's narrator explains that, being from a small island, he had come to London looking for size. He ended up with the feeling that he had come at the wrong time. Grandeur was a thing of the past; he had come too late. Moreover, his expectations came from Dickens, the dark city evoked but never described in Dickens, and therefore he felt underread, ignorant. In his youth, to look ahead, to travel outward, to expand, meant going to England. When he finally got there, he was surprised by a familiar feeling, one he had known back in Trinidad, that of being in the wrong place. Nevertheless, he dedicated himself to becoming what he called a metropolitan writer, by which he meant a writer whose material would enable him to display a particular kind of personality.

Some of the sternest narrators of the late twentieth century have come out of the English-speaking Caribbean. Derek Walcott is now the old softie of the region, with his love of learning, his love for his comrades in poetry, the still-mourned Lowell, the much-missed Brodsky. In *A Small Island,* the arctic eye of Jamaica Kincaid guides the flame of her prose over the library and her Church of England education on Antigua, as if to say that for her generation there would be no falling for the wish to arrive, and that anyway London was no longer the center of things, culturally, for every West Indian. In *The European Tribe,* Phillips also repudiates the ambition to belong to this center.

If Englishness is undesirable, and black Britishness yet impossible, Phillips tells us what as a young man he put in its place. His internationalism was derived from the African American writers of his supplementary reading. *The European Tribe* is loaded with epigrams. If Phillips is in Spain, then the footprints that he indicates he is aware of are those of Richard Wright. If he is in France, then he is following Claude McKay. And of course he found Baldwin at home—*en ma Provençe*, my rose, says the poem. They who back home had been accused of abandoning their people were welcomed by black Europeans of Phillips's generation as heralds. They taught them how to turn feeling dispossessed into a cultural advantage, a point of view.

In 1976, Phillips was lifting his head to catch news of the riots in Notting Hill and the British press woke to the problem of black urban youth. But nowhere in *The European Tribe* does he make any mention of C. L. R. James. James paid a price for his Marxism, as did Du Bois for his enemy-of-my-enemyism. Dear, old Marxism. Those African American writers whom we so admire—several of them would not have found their way into print when they did had it not been for the Marxist press and Left intelligentsia. In the West, what it meant to be a Marxist or a Communist changed from revelation to revelation, era to era, even for blacks, though the thousands who swooned over the speech patterns of Angela Davis, when she was attacked for being the high yellow princess of Brezhnevism, did not think of her as such. When Phillips was leaving Oxford, an interest in and identification with black America could take its place. The civil rights movement remains a radicalism that has not lost its prestige through all the attacks by neoconservatives and members of the Christian Right on liberal, humanist culture.

George Lamming, in *The Pleasures of Exile,* published in 1960, says that the West Indian Negro who sets out on a journey of cultural discovery to Africa will be insecure, because his relation to the continent is so personal and problematic. His status as a man gives a clear indication of the reason for the departure of his ancestors from Africa. That migration was a commercial deportation, not a chosen act. Then, too, even though, as his West Indian friends in Washington, D.C., would have no trouble convincing him, to be black in the United States was to wake prepared, as for an emergency, nevertheless the Negro in America had in all likelihood been introduced somehow to African history. But the education of the West Indian "did not provide him with any reading to rummage through as a guide to the lost kingdoms of names and places which give geography a human significance. He knows it through rumor and myth which is made sinister by a foreign tutelage, and he becomes, through the gradual conditioning of his education, identified with fear: fear of that continent as a world beyond human intervention."

Yet when Lamming landed in the heat of Accra in 1958, a procession of Boy Scouts, there to welcome some dignitary, took him back in his mind to West Indian children celebrating an important occasion in their village. And he saw himself in every detail of them—until after the ceremony, when the procession broke apart into boys speaking either Fanti or Ga. English was a way of thinking when the situation required it, but otherwise "they owed Prospero no debt of language." Lamming felt that next to Ghana the West Indies were backward, because Ghana had its independence, its freedom.

In Phillips's most recent book, *The Atlantic Sound,* a work of nonfiction, the optimism of the days of independence in Africa might as well be as remote as the time of Mandeville. Phillips's American-found internationalism will confront what he sees as the romanticism of Pan-Africanism among African Americans themselves. However, his immediate purpose is to visit the points of the Triangular Trade— Liverpool in England, Elmina in Ghana, Charleston in South Carolina—and to reflect on the human organization of the centuries of this traffic in brass, cloth, gold, Africans, rum, tobacco, rice, cotton. C. L. R. James will figure at last, alongside Langston Hughes and other black American wonderers about Africa. No doubt Phillips means to evoke Richard Wright's *Black Power,* his account of his disillusioning visit to Ghana when it was called the Gold Coast, in 1953. But Naipaul springs more often to mind.

Not so long ago, Phillips poured scorn over Naipaul for the letters that the gifted young writer sent home from Oxford to his heroic father trapped in that despised place, Trinidad. Phillips cannot abide the disdain involved in Naipaul's distanced self. However, in *The Atlantic Sound,* Phillips sometimes takes a tone often associated with Naipaul the reporter: disagreeable, full of head shaking. A dandy sits at the bar, annoyed with his First World ass for his self-imposed mission among the believers. But this critical disposition is a form of protection, a guard against being taken in, a way of preserving the integrity of the enterprise. The brief Phillips gives himself is clear: to mystify nothing, not to be seduced into poetic ambivalence. He must decide, based only on what he sees, and he will see only what he sees.

When *The Atlantic Sound* opens, Phillips is in Guadeloupe, meeting the first of his drivers and minders. He has come a long way as a personage since *The European Tribe*. Phillips says to his Creole escort that he has "sort of" been on a ship before. "I do not want to have to explain to him that forty years ago my parents travelled by ship from the Caribbean to England with me, their four-month old son, as hand luggage." His escort is more concerned that Phillips realizes his ship is a banana boat that actually takes cargo. The ship at the quay is Liberian registered, has German officers in sandals and brown socks, a Burmese cabin steward, and less than a dozen British, German, and American passengers. The versatile ship carries cars, trucks, containers, and is refrigerated for the transportation of fruit. "I am eagerly calculating how many days I will have to endure until I return to Britain. . . . For me this will not be an Atlantic crossing into the unknown. I fully understand the world that will greet me at the end of the journey."

A day on a freighter is long. There are rum parties in the bar to alleviate the boredom. After three days, they dock in Limon, a down-at-heels coastal port in Costa Rica. Two days later, they are in Guatemala. The captain entertains Phillips with his old hand's tales. "In 1963 in Chile, I walked into a bar that was full of goddamn ex-Nazis. On the jukebox there were Nazi songs, and these bastards were trying to marry off their daughters to me." The Straits of Florida go by, the wind howls, the ship pitches and rolls, the smell of ripening fruit is overwhelming. Phillips says that he once asked his mother what she did on the ship to England in 1958. She said she worked out how to get to the lifeboats with him in her arms and her eyes closed.

"As I continue to stare at the porpoises playing in the strong light of dawn, I now know how she and all the other emigrants felt as they crossed the Atlantic Ocean: they felt lonely."

After two weeks at sea, the revered white cliffs of Dover are in sight. "I understand. I have arrived. I imagine—desire—closure." And so *The Atlantic Sound* begins with an ending, as if to say what follows is not personal. By temperament, it would seem,

Phillips is opposed to what in his prologue he must do as a first-person narrator, especially a black one: explain, identify himself. Who am I? I am none of your business; but you, they, it are my business. Perhaps this tone is his way of saying that nothing is more personal than an individual's ideas.

Leaving home:

> The African dispatches the money to the white man and his African heart swells with pride. The African hopes for a new dawn; a brighter future. Luck has not been on his side. For many years now there have been problems. But, with the help of the white man, he can once again become great. Time passes. The white man is silent. African voices begin to whisper. The African is consumed with anxiety. And then he discovers himself to be floundering in a place of despair. He remembers

that not all white men are honest. He remembers that not all white men are de-
cent. Again he hears African voices.
Friends are whispering. Enemies are
laughing. He is still powerful, but this ill
fortune heralds the beginning of the end.
For many years the African has been re-
spected. But now the white man has
cheated him of nearly everything he owns.
Abandoning his Christian beliefs, he
makes desperate sacrifices to native Gods.
But they have forgotten him. His life is
running aground. The African has dis-
patched money to the white man. And
now his heart is heavy with grief.

Phillips retells the story of John Emmanuel
Ocansey as a parable of betrayal. In 1881, John
E. Ocansey traveled from the Gold Coast to
Liverpool, on sensitive business for William
Narh Ocansey, a long-established trader in

palm oil who was both John Ocansey's adopted
father and father-in-law. The industrial revo-
lution had increased the value of palm oil, because it was used for soap and to keep machin-
ery going. The Ocansey family processed palm
oil at its factories along the Upper Volta, then
transported it in floating casks down river to
vessels that would take it to England. In 1879,
William Narh Ocansey contracted with an
agent in Liverpool, Robert W. Hickson, for the
building of a steam launch, a smoking canoe,
in order to reduce the risk to his cargo on the
fast-flowing rivers. He sent from Addah an
order and enough palm oil to cover the cost of
constructing the vessel.

After several delays and empty reassur-
ances, Ocansey sent his son-in-law to Liverpool to discover what had happened to the
ship he ordered and the goods and money he
had sent. The twists of the British legal system
left John Ocansey with lots of time in which to

walk the streets. He published his observa-
tions, *African Trading; or the Trials of William
Narh Ocansey,* in Liverpool in 1881. Phillips
makes use of Ocansey's account and novelizes
the historical experience. This is the sort of
character Phillips has used before in his fiction: the complicit African, the Christianized
black, the tribal isolato, the guy who could
write in English. Phillips enters Ocansey's
feelings when he takes leave of his wife and
young child. He has Ocansey explain his cau-
tion around strangers, white and black, his re-
lief when missionaries board, religious services being one ritual he can participate in
without too great a fear of rebuff and without
too much need to talk about himself. As
Ocansey travels along the west coast of Africa,
then strikes out for the Canaries, Phillips in-
tersperses another story, that of the history of
the Atlantic trade and the rapid, drastic
growth of Liverpool as a port.

Safely arrived in Liverpool, not sold off into servitude as he had half feared he would be, Ocansey finds lodgings with a stout, honest woman. His father's agents, Hickson, Lyle & Co., are bankrupt. A meeting of their creditors will take place in June. Meanwhile, Ocansey gathers his impressions. He becomes acquainted with Liverpudlians who also love the Wesleyan service. But

John was increasingly careful about those homes that he was prepared to enter. It was not that he lacked a desire to mix among these Liverpudlians, for clearly by doing so he was learning much about their society, and about England in general, and he imagined that his information would be useful to him in his future trading life. However, John understood that there were certain attitudes about Africans which still prevailed in this city, attitudes which were at best uncomfortable, at worst insulting, and he had no desire to put himself into a position where he had either to defend his people, or chastise his hosts for their uncivilized behavior.

To get satisfaction from Hickson, Ocansey must go to court. The charges against Hickson are that he entered into a false contract and that he converted money to his own use in violation of good faith. The Liverpool Assizes is convened with much ceremony in July, and Ocansey follows the proceedings as best he can. In the end, Hickson pleads not guilty to the first charge, the more serious of the two, and is acquitted. He is found guilty of the second. The judge sentences him to fifteen months' hard labor. But the settlement gives the Ocanseys very little of the capital they had risked. Exhausted, frustrated, Ocansey knows that it is time to go. He has had a letter from Africa informing him of his grandmother's death.

Present but unspoken throughout Phillips's version of Ocansey's sojourn is the arrogance behind the loose business practices of English traders, as well as the embarrassment that an African is taking the law seriously. Phillips's own journey to Liverpool, to the scene of mercantile fast ones and judicial curve balls, he treats in a postscript of total disgust.

I first sensed that there was something disturbing about Liverpool when, as an eleven year old boy, I stood on the terraces watching my team, Leeds United, play against the Liverpool-based club, Everton. At that time Everton, in common with most football clubs in England, possessed no non-white players. In fact, when the occasional non-white player did have the temerity to run onto an English

football pitch, he would invariably be
subjected to a volley of racist baying.
Every time he touched the ball the crowd
would erupt in anger, and it was ex-
tremely common for bananas to be
thrown at black players. Such was Britain
in the sixties and seventies.

In the early eighties, Liverpool had its race
riot, in Toxteth, Liverpool 8. In the nineties,
nonwhite faces were at last on display at football matches. "I did not recognize this suspi-
ciously multiracial Liverpool."

Phillips meets a twenty-three-year-old
whose passion is the city's hidden history,
meaning its black history. The BBC had sent
the young man to make a personal documen-
tary about going home—to Elmina in Ghana,
which contains one of the very best preserved
slave forts, "a place which reminds us of
where we came from," the tense young man

says. This is the first of the sort of tip-off that sends Phillips to the next point on his compass. "I have met young men like this before, intelligent men who exist in a liminal zone where the line between creativity and self-destruction is etched vaguely into the sand." He is appalled by the young man's anti-Semitism. In *The European Tribe,* Phillips recalls Isak Dinesen's irritation in *Out of Africa* that no matter what she said she could not turn her African houseboy against Shylock. The young man tells Phillips that he can trace his family back to 1842. He is proud to be a LBB, Liverpool Born Black. He explains that LBBs and blacks from elsewhere don't get along, but Phillips just sees the black neighborhood, Liverpool 8, as boarded up and poor, regardless of where the people come from.

He visits St. George's Hall, the setting for Ocansey's trial, but is allowed only a glimpse of the great mosaic floor. There is a permanent exhibition on slavery in the Maritime Museum and then there are the abandoned Albert Docks, where Phillips sits and remembers his first reading of *Wuthering Heights.* Mr. Earnshaw comes down one morning in 1771 dressed for a journey, the walk to Liverpool. Three days later, Mr. Earnshaw opens his greatcoat to offer his wife "a gift of God, though it's as dark almost as if it came from the devil." The black-haired, ragged child, speaking some gibberish nobody could understand, is Heathcliff. There is no textual evidence, Phillips says, of Heathcliff's black lineage. He is called gypsy, dusky, Lascar, an American or Spanish castaway, but what else, Phillips now asks himself, could Brontë have had in mind about this urchin found near the infamous docks? "I am glad that I am leaving. It is disquieting to be in a place where history is so physically present, yet so glaringly absent from people's consciousness. But where is it any different? Maybe this is the modern condition, and Liverpool is merely acting out this reality with an honest vigor."

Homeward bound.

On the flight to Ghana, a whisky-soaked West African businessman asks Phillips, Where are you from? It is the question, "the problem question for those of us who have grown up in societies which define themselves by excluding others. Usually us. A coded question. Are you one of us? Are you one of ours? . . . Where are you really from?. . . Does he mean, who am I? Does he mean, do I belong?. . . He listens, and then he spoils it all. 'So, my friend, you are going home to Africa. To Ghana.' I say nothing. *No, I am not going home,*" is his emphatic, italicized thought. But when his fellow passenger falls asleep, Phillips concedes that he envies him his rootedness.

He is met in humid Accra by Mohammed Mansour Nassirudeen, a youngish man whose story is in part already familiar to Phillips. Not long before, Nassirudeen had been deported from Britain. He'd been a student and had overstayed his visa. He'd resisted deportation, because of the disgrace of going back to Ghana with nothing to show for his eight years away, not even a degree. He will become part of what Phillips calls the stubborn predictability of Third World travel. He wants to live in America, even as an illegal immigrant, and he would like help from Phillips.

Nassirudeen, born in proud Kumasi in 1961, has a galling story that takes him from four A levels in Islamic Studies, Government, Economics, and the General Paper to trying to be one of the family breadwinners after his father's death in 1975. There is terrifying, oil-boom Lagos in his story, contractual work in oil-boom Libya, dangerous work in indifferent Saudi

Arabia, and a correspondence course in business law at the University of Oklahoma, which he doesn't complete because of an older brother's death in Cairo. How to get out of the Arab world, the Soviet bloc? Because of all the Libyan stamps in his passport, he threw it away.

He got to London via Belgrade. His student working visa meant that Nassirudeen could pick strawberries in Peterborough, but after three months he was supposed to leave. He didn't. His English life conformed to a pattern: enrollment in a school, London University, for instance, a job stacking shelves in a supermarket at night or delivering pizzas, and some room in a friend of a friend's house. He hung on, got out of scrapes with the authorities in 1988, and again in 1990, but his luck ran out in 1994 when he was denounced by a colleague to the Home Office. The indignities he suffered in detention were many. "Perhaps it was wrong that I should be in any way judging this man who had not the opportunities that I had." Nassirudeen's neediness hovers around Phillips everywhere in Ghana.

Nassirudeen waits outside while Phillips visits a Ghanaian playwright, a renowned Pan-Africanist, who explains that not long after the first slave ships set sail the idea took hold that those of Africa and those of African origins overseas constituted a family with a broken history. The idea was seized upon with enthusiasm by those who discovered in the Americas that they were not white. The discovery engendered in them a romantic yearning, and although they would be in a place where the language, climate, and culture were foreign, because they would be free of the stigma of race they would at least be home. His Pan-Africanism is a simple concept about the solidarity and cohesion of Africans and people of African descent. "We have to rescue the continuity of values from our past."

Much got thrown away because of the intrusions of Europe and the resulting Eurocentric Africans who did not know who they were. It is not a question of going back to something as much as it is one of moving ahead.

Nassirudeen again waits outside as Phillips looks up a South Carolina-born—there's another tip-off—African American dentist. He had been a classmate of Nkrumah's at Lincoln University in Pennsylvania and in 1956 moved to the Gold Coast, where he set up practice. He is proud that he has always had a skill to offer his new home. He is also proud that he knew them all—Du Bois, C. L. R. James, George Padmore, Richard Wright, Maya Angelou, Frantz Fanon, John Henrik Clarke. The philosophical dentist tells Phillips that he has never pretended to be anything other than what he is, an African American. Of the African American seekers who want to settle permanently to Elmina, he says, "I have no romance. I know what it's like to live without a television or a toilet but they don't. The States has let them down in some way and they expect Africa to solve their problems for them. Africa isn't ready to do that. And maybe they're not ready for Africa."

And so Phillips and an anxious Nassirudeen head for Elmina. Along the way there is little scenery. They pass the "Don't Tell Your Wife" Bar, the "Lover Boy" Hair Salon. Cardboard shacks alternate with new five-storey buildings with ATMs. There's the "Professor Classic Baldhead" Barbers, the "Sober Spot" Bar, the "Oasis of Love" Travel and Tours, and a weight-loss center, the "Figure Correction Shop." Phillips concentrates instead on the history of Elmina, called A Mina or The Mine by the Portuguese who were trading for gold in the late fifteenth century. A fortified castle was ordered built by John II, and Portuguese scribes left a description of his envoy Diego de

Azambuja meeting what he thought was an African king, but who in all probability was an important merchant, at the mouth of the River Benya, where the fortress was to be raised.

Elmina changed in nature, and became independent of its Akan neighbors both economically and in terms of its character. It rapidly became a large, multi-ethnic, multilingual place of trade which included people of mixed descent. Not only were there those whose fathers were European, but there were those whose fathers and mothers were of different African ethnic origins. Unlike the pro-Fante Cape Coast, some twenty miles to the east, heterogeneous Elmina managed to be both pro-Fante and pro-Asante, so that when conflict eventually erupted between these two great inland empires, Elmina was the one place on the coast where relative peace reigned.

By the middle of the sixteenth century, it was clear that the really important commodity on the West African coast was human beings.

"Prepare to be swept away by the romance of home," Phillips tells himself, installed in a hotel bungalow in Elmina. He has come for Panafest, a time when the diasporan family celebrates the achievements of the Pan-African world. And Phillips is scathing, absolutely scathing, about the disappointments of Panafest, the poor performances, the cobbled-together rituals, the overblown rhetoric, and the Jamaicans who drive the hotel desk clerk to the brink by cooking in their rooms, blowing dope in their rooms, inviting anyone up to their rooms, pulling the lemon grass outside their windows to make tea, when the lemon grass should be there to help keep away mosquitoes. And he is equally outraged by the small-islandness of a "floodlighting ceremony" at another slave fortress, Cape

Coast Castle. Nassirudeen is no less discomforted.

Back in Elmina, Phillips meets a forty-five-year-old African American from Westchester County who, after graduating from Georgia State College in 1975, enrolled in the Hasadbah Yisrael Congregation in Brooklyn and then the House of David House of Study, also in Brooklyn. The Hebrew Israelites see themselves in the tradition of Rabbi Josiah Ford, Marcus Garvey's music director. There is even a community, founded in 1969, of two thousand Hebrew Israelites in the Negev desert in Israel. Catch the tip-off, the human link. However, this Westchester gentleman's group was detained at the airport in Tel Aviv in 1986. The Israelis were afraid they would try to settle permanently. So in 1987 he and sixteen other African Americans followed new signs and were delivered to Elmina. Ghana, he tells Phillips, is the gateway to Africa for African Americans. "Why do you think white people are here? They can see that Africa has virtues." But after dismal Panafest, Phillips wonders why the Hebrew Israelite can't see that: Africa is not a cure; Africa is not a psychiatrist.

Home.

Phillips leaves Nassirudeen sitting on a plastic chair and—so abruptly—we next find him in Charleston, South Carolina, on a hot afternoon, seeking out the enemies and friends of Federal Judge J. Waties Waring. Born into a distinguished white South Carolina family, Waring changed discriminatory practices in his courtroom, appointed the first black bailiff in the state, and then in 1947 upheld in a landmark case the NAACP's contention that segregated political primaries were unconstitutional. After the 1948 election, Waring and his second wife were ostracized by Charleston society. Their only comfort was to be had on the black side of town and they became so identified with blacks and the struggle for equal rights, so famous in their time for it, that they were threatened, stoned, phoned, and attacked. Phillips looks for their witnesses and he also searches for Sullivan Island, that corral where slaves were "seasoned." It is an overgrown lot, silent, like all the other places where Phillips has gone to hear the past speak.

His message is direct, if not simple: the past is a book. The past can only talk in a book. Otherwise, all is a landscape, a profoundly altered landscape. In an epilogue to *The Atlantic Sound,* Phillips has made the journey to the community of the Hebrew Israelites in the Negev. Fortunately, they themselves mention Jonestown first. To them, their message isn't religious, it is spiritual. But Phillips sees them as misguided folk who have come home to a land they can't tame, to a world that doesn't recognize them. It is a closed society, this utopia, "the final irony of life in the great captivity," as the group members, mostly from Chicago, refer to the United States. "There is no closure. There will be no closure. . . .You were transported in a wooden vessel across a broad expanse of water to a place which rendered your tongue silent. Look. Listen. Learn. And as you began to speak, you remembered fragments of a former life. Shards of memory. Careful. Some will draw blood." A Zimbabwean writer once told Phillips that the sea carries Africa on its back like an island.

The Atlantic Sound is not a travel book. It is about the impossibility of retracing the steps of the Triangular Trade, of the middle passage. The past is a book, and while at Cape Coast Castle Phillips invokes the figure of Philip Quaque, the African-born, London-educated chaplain of the slave fort there from 1766 to 1816. For over fifty years, Quaque wrote letters to his sponsors in London, the Society for the Propagation of the Gospel in Foreign Parts, about his disappointments with his school for

Africans, about his frustration trying to minister to Europeans, who wanted only to drink, be polygamous, get rich, and survive. It puzzles Phillips how Quaque could have lived in the Cape Coast Castle all those decades and never once mentioned the Africans, his brothers, held in the cells directly below his living quarters.

But it is also puzzling that Phillips, if he can't bear the actuality of Panafest, doesn't talk about Pan-Africanism as the history of an idea, he who demands such consciousness of the people of Liverpool. Alexander Crummell, Edward Blyden, George Padmore, Kwame Anthony Appiah—no, Phillips will not be really engaged. Perhaps that long-ago first trip to the Caribbean used up his journey-of-return ration.[1]

He does not go to Du Bois's grave in Ghana. He refuses to make his trip a pilgrimage. He has a right to stand outside of that feeling, but it is as though he cannot afford to be moved. "I interviewed some fellow visitors as they emerged from the dungeons into the sunlit courtyard," we read in Henry Louis Gates's *Wonders of the African World,* "where they posed for photographs by the Gate of Tears, the infamous portal through which slaves boarded the ships bound for the New World. Why had they come? What did they expect to find, on this return to our putative homeland? What did this place make them feel? Sheer horror and deepest rage at European brutality was the shared answer. They had come to indict the European oppressors and to experience the awful point of departure where Africans became African Americans."

Phillips is a recessive presence in his narrative. Excerpts from books or letters by blacks in history who had dealings with England seem to take his place, to stand in for him, to speak for him, which adds to the sense of an unaddressed anger and horror and antispirituality throughout. The section about Ocansey and Liverpool

Phillips calls "Leaving Home," and that title has a dual meaning. The section about Nassirudeen and Elmina Phillips calls "Homeward Bound," and that, as it turns out, will have a deceptive meaning. But the section on Waring and Charleston, where Phillips had never been and where he knew no one, is called "Home." *The Atlantic Sound* is a long and bitter farewell to England. He's off. He's gone. He's New World now. The metropolis, the source, has moved. The mother country is the outpost now.

> *Ca Ca Caliban*
> *get a new master, be a new man.*

Notes

1. Phillips takes up this and similar points in his recent collection of essays, *A New World Order* (London: Secker & Warburg, 2001; New York: Knopf, 2002).

Acknowledgments

I WANT TO THANK THE DU BOIS Institute for the honor of the invitation to appear in its lecture series named for Alain Locke. I am particularly grateful to Nina Kollars of the Afro-American Studies department at Harvard for her patience and graceful efficiency. I must also thank Craig Raine, fellow, New College, Oxford, for his helpful remarks about Kipling; and Judith Thurman, for her willingness to answer questions concerning Rogers's assertions about Cleopatra and the Ptolemies. Ever since the present chairman of the Afro-American Studies department at Harvard unveiled what he calls the trope of the Talking Book in *The Signifying Monkey*, he has done so much through his writings and teaching to expand and deepen the field of African American studies. That so much is now in print, that there is so much to study and to know, is due in no small part to his energy and inspiration. He is a brilliant and generous soul, Henry Louis Gates, Jr. I thank him and I thank you for coming to these talks.

The Alain LeRoy Locke Lectures were
established in 1999 to honor
Alain LeRoy Locke (1886–1954),
the godfather of the Harlem Renaissance.
Sponsored by the Perseus Books Group,
these lectures are intended to honor
the memory and contributions of this noted
Harvard scholar, who became the first and,
until 1963, only African American to win a
Rhodes Scholarship to Oxford.